THE IMPOSSIBILITIES OF SOCIAL DEMOCRACY

To my friend
and comrade
A. BARTELL

THE IMPOSSIBILITIES OF SOCIAL DEMOCRACY

VERNON RICHARDS

"A wise man neither lets himself be governed nor seeks to govern others; he wishes that reason should govern alone and always."

LA BRUYÈRE (1688)

LONDON
FREEDOM PRESS
1978

First Published
1978
by FREEDOM PRESS
84b Whitechapel High St
London E.1.

ISBN: 0 900384 16 6

Printed by Bookmag, Henderson Road, Inverness

CONTENTS

A somewhat cynical proverb current among the Rumanian peasants, who say that "only fools exult when Governments change."
LONDON TIMES (19 NOV. 1928)

*"When change of rulers happens to a state
'Tis but a change of name unto the poor"*
PHAEDRUS: Fables (C. 25 B.C.)

INTRODUCTION

The title of this collection of political articles originally published in the anarchist journal *Freedom* was suggested to me on reading the text of a lecture given by Bernard Shaw in 1891 to his fellow Fabians, with the title *The Impossibilities of Anarchism.* From the very outset Shaw was at pains to point out that his criticism was "confined to the practical measures proposed by Anarchists, and raises no discussion as to aims or principles". Anarchist methods (and they did not include terrorism incendiarism or thieving) were criticised as being so idealistic and impractical as to be "impossible". For progress, he said, could not be made "without the gravest violations of principles of all sorts" including the recognition of the State and "compromise at every step".

It cannot be denied that the Social Democrats by following Shaw's advice have made considerable progress in their quest for political power. After all they have been the government of this country twice albeit briefly in the inter-war years (1924 1929) but no less than five times since 1945, with an overwhelming majority in 1945 and a large one in 1966. They have been in office for some 17 years in the past 33 and for 11 in the past 14 years. How nearer are we now to Socialism than we were in 1891?

Then, Bernard Shaw was denouncing the conflict between "ideal Socialism and practical Social Democracy" which he claimed destroyed the Chartist organisation "as it destroyed the Socialist League only the other day. But it had never gone so far as the conflict between Social-Democracy and Anarchism". He attacked the anarchists for advocating abstention from voting and refusal to pay taxes when his fellow Social Democrats were seeking to persuade workers to organise their votes for the "right" candidates and to press for the taxation of unearned income to finance schools and libraries and the nationalisation of industries!

Peter Townsend and other contemporary Labour supporters have pointed out on more than one occasion that in the affluent society, even with a Labour government, the rich have been getting richer and the poor poorer. Everything is relative, it is true, and today's "poverty" would probably have seemed like affluence to the socialists and anarchists of the last century. However, the social democrats can claim no credit for this. It was achieved by sacrificing 50 million young lives in two world wars which they supported, their leaders joining coalition governments on both occasions in spite of their professed Internationalism*. But then progress calls for "compromise at every step" and the wars did spark off a technological revolution as well as social upheavals the like of which Shaw's Fabians could not have visualised even in their least unimaginative moments. And how did the social democrats react?

They allowed the capitalists to exploit the technical revolution, content to tail after the Unions echoing their demands for more production and more money (for their members), more goods and public services, mere lackeys of capitalism. And those social upheavals all ended in disaster mainly because of the political timidity everywhere of social democrats who obviously preferred Fascism, Nazism and Franco to revolution.

The volume has been divided into four parts each representing what for this writer is a major "impossibility" of social democracy.

The first is that Labour Party 'Socialism' has very little in common with socialism even as professed by the Fabians in the 1890s or by a Tawney in the '20s or an Attlee in the '30s.

The second is that what I call 'Bevanism' is not an ideological struggle, a battle for the soul of socialism but a sordid struggle for power by ambitious professional politicians, vain men and women eager to taste the fruits of office or even simply the limelight which our insatiable media are only too glad to turn onto any political exhibitionist willing to defy the party whip and upset the head-counting ritual in a vote of confidence. And the more the Labour Party establishes itself as the party of government and less the party of socialism so it attracts ambitious power-seeking professionals, glib performers, tongue-in-cheek 'socialists', using Parliament as a stepping stone for their business careers and for personal ambitions.

Atlee has pointed out that before the 1914-18 war all Labour candidates were men of "working class parentage and predominantly of T.U. officials". It was not until 1922 that the first Labour candidate with a middle class background was elected. Times *have* changed!

*Attlee even suggests in *The Labour Party in Perspective* (London 1937) that the growth of the Labour Party in the 1920s would not have been so rapid had there not been a war in 1914.

The betrayal of Ramsay MacDonald and his friends in 1931 is still remembered as a major disaster. Attlee admirably sums up the corroding effect of power on the very first secretary general of the Labour Party when he writes of MacDonald

> He had for some years been more and more attracted by the social environment of the well to do classes. He had got more and more out of touch with the rank and file of the Party, while the adulation which is almost inseparable from the necessary publicity given to the leader of a great movement had gone to his head and increased his natural vanity. The philosophy of gradualness which he had always maintained became almost indistinguishable from Conservatism.

Today such betrayals are a commonplace. Think of the ex-ministers and M.P.s who were once boosted as the dedicated standard bearers of Labour Party socialism and who ended up in big business and/or the Tory camp: Hartley Shawcross, Alfred Robens, Christopher Mayhew, George Brown, Ray Gunter, John Stonehouse, Woodrow Wyatt, Richard Marsh, Reg Prentice, to name a few that immediately come to mind.

And there was Bernard Shaw, ninety-odd years ago, saying how simple it would be to introduce socialism by getting the right people into Parliament, his argument being that since all orders "come ultimately from the State — meaning in this country the House of Commons" then

> a House consisting of 660 gentlemen and 10 workmen will order the soldier to take money from the people for the landlords. A House of Commons consisting of 660 workmen and 10 gentlemen will probably, unless the 660 are fools, order the soldier to take money from the landlords for the people. With that hint I leave the matter in the full conviction that the State, in spite of the Anarchists, will continue to be used against the people by the classes until it is used by the people against the classes with equal ability and equal resolution.

Yes, *by the people* but the 660 politicians in the House of Commons are not the people but their rulers whether they be ex-workmen or gentlemen.

The third "impossibility" to be dealt with is the Trades Unions, the dog that wags the (Labour Party) tail. It is quite obvious from the uninformed attacks on the Unions as the tail that wags the dog that most critics do not realise that the Labour Party was started in 1906 with a group of Trade Unionists being elected to Parliament with the specific task of supporting organised Labour by action in the political field, and though the Party is no longer "a mere political expression of Trades Unionism" the fact remains that the Unions through the political levy and the substantial donations they make to the Party's election fund and other special appeals, are the Party's main source of income. And who pays the piper must surely call the tune most of the time.

If the Unions were politically radical their influence and power not in the money markets or the Stock Exchange but at the source of real wealth production, could not be other than beneficial to the cause of socialism. But their structure and function almost inevitably make them reactionary hierarchical establishment organisations. As Malatesta put it

All movements founded on material and immediate interests (and a mass working class movement cannot be founded on anything else), if the ferment, the drive and the unremitting efforts of men of ideas struggling and making sacrifices for an ideal future are lacking, tend to adapt themselves to circumstances, foster a conservative spirit, and the fear of change in those who manage to improve their conditions, and often end up by creating new privileged classes and serving to support and consolidate the system which one would want to destroy.

Attlee makes some shrewd observations on the duality of the role of the unions.

There are Unions in which the everyday work is so much a matter of co-operation with the employers that their leaders tend to forget or ignore the ultimate aims of the movement. They have become so constitutional that they are in essence Conservative. There have been instances, on the other hand, of the capture of Unions by extremists who have, by a policy of continual strife, ultimately ruined the organisation because they constantly exacted from their members sacrifices which should not have been demanded except on some major issue.

The fourth "impossibility" is the Means. However democratically elections are conducted their purpose is authoritarian: to decide which bunch of politicians will be our rulers. To secure a majority of votes the major parties must appeal not to the extremist fringes but to the 'solid majority', to the lowest common denominator of demands and issues. And the result of playing this electoral game for so long is that the means have become the ends. Socialism has been sacrificed to the struggle for office and power.

Colchester July 1978 V.R.

All the articles in this volume were published as unsigned editorals in the anarchist journal *Freedom.* Hence the editoral "we" which at most committed the then editorial group.

I have not been tempted to update the articles with footnotes and contemporary illustrations because I feel that if anything meaningful emerges from them it is surely the conclusion that *plus ça change* . . . that nothing in the party political game, the power struggle, has changed except the names of the performers, and the intelligent, politically informed reader will, I am sure, have no difficulty in doing his/her own updating.

I have given the date of publication of each article and unless otherwise stated press reports of speeches and events were taken from the then *Manchester Guardian,* a better source of real news than its National successor.

A fact that the reader should keep at the back of his mind if he wishes to get the full flavour of the hyprocrisy of party politics and its practitioners, is that during all the years covered by these articles *the Tories were in power* and *the Labour Party 'socialists' in opposition!*

"It is a fact that Anarchists and Socialists have always profoundly disagreed in their concepts of historic evolution and the revolutionary crises that this evolution creates, and consequently they have hardly ever been in agreement on the means to adopt, or the opportunities that have existed from time to time to open up the way towards human emancipation.

But this is only an incidental and minor disagreement. There have always been socialists who have been in a hurry, just as there are also anarchists who want to advance with leaden feet, and even some who do not believe at all in revolution. The important, fundamental dissension is quite another: Socialists are authoritarians, anarchists are libertarians".

E. MALATESTA (1921)

1
Labour Party "Socialism"

A BENIGN BIG BROTHER?

One has only to read the first pages of the Labour Party's "policy pamphlet" on Personal Freedom to realise that there is no connection between contents and title. What is offered and proposed are a series of legal safeguards for the individual (or what is left of him), against abuses by the officers of government and the representatives of the State. In *Personal Freedom** the Labour Party is not putting forward principles of freedom and suggesting methods for their attainment; it is in fact seeking to adjust the individual to an acceptance of the State as the spear-head of freedom by the trick of offering him means for disputing the legality of the actions of the Executive.

To provide the individual with the legal machinery to defend himself against the abuses of power is not freedom; at most it is simply a means for keeping the authority of the Executive within bounds. Authority, by definition, is the denial of individual freedom; to legislate for freedom is either a contradiction in terms or has meaning only when the word "freedom" has none.

This Labour Party pamphlet is the first of a series of policy statements following the Party's decision at its last Conference to use the three years before the next elections for "serious re-thinking" of its aims and principles. Far from injecting new life into the Party's thinking, this statement of policy is a kind of funeral oration over the dead body of "democratic socialism". (And sub-consciously the producers of this pamphlet must have thought likewise when they

*Personal Freedom. Labour's Policy for the Individual and Society (Labour Party, 1956, 32 pp. 9d.)

designed a cover in which black predominates).

> The Labour Party aims at a society resting upon the following basis: (1) Concentration of power — military, political and economic — should serve, and be seen to serve, the whole community, and not dominate it; (2) Privileges of the few must be transformed into rights, available to every citizen; (3) A fairer distribution of wealth and opportunity must be advanced by positive State action, with the assistance of a free trade union and co-operative movement; (4) Effective civil liberties and an independent judiciary must safeguard personal freedom against abuse of power, either by the State or by any organisation...
> We believe that the only political framework within which a free society can flourish is that of parliamentary democracy with full rights of opposition.

The Labour Party believes, to quote again, that "the State is made for man, not man for the State". Such unbelievable beliefs spring from the idea that though the authority of the State can "damage personal freedom" it can, nevertheless "be used to extend freedom in a very real sense". The Labour movement since its beginnings has "clearly not regarded State action as the only means of social progress" and

> ... self-help within groups independent of the State was an objective of early socialists [nevertheless] State action was necessary to provide conditions in which the groups of individuals could properly function ... In various ways ... the British people have extended their freedoms both by action within groups and directly through the State.

The example we are given of "necessary State action" is of "the Acts ... passed, not only to make trade unions lawful, but to grant them certain legal rights necessary to their practical operation". On a later page, however, we are told that in the "quiet social revolution that has been taking place" since the birth of the Labour Party half a century ago: *"the trade unions, after a long struggle, have won their place as an indispensable part of the nation"* What a miserable end after such a long struggle!

We think the dishonesty of the argument here is quite clear. On the one hand they argue that it was the passing of the Acts by the State which made it possible for the trade unions to operate; on the other, where, for party propaganda purposes, they want to boost the achievements of the Labour movement, they stress the *long struggle* of the trade unions, and refer to the place *they have won.*

Governments have only two ways of dealing with powerful unofficial organisations in their midst. If they feel strong enough they suppress them legally; otherwise they seek to contain or even absorb them into the State machine. Obviously the latter method is the best since the Government kills two birds with the one stone: it passes off as democratic and the unofficial organisation is tamed and controlled.*.

Today the Tory Government looks upon the Trade Union movement as a vital part of the economic system. Not as a force which threatens, but on the contrary, as a pillar of capitalism which is what the Labour Party means when it refers to the trade unions as "an indispensable part of the nation".

The Labour Party's apologia for the State is understandable since their objective is to take over the reins of power and, by legislation, taxation, death-duties, the replacement of private- by public-control, carry out a programme of social and economic reform, aiming at "equality" and the "classless society". The State will be a kind of benign Big Brother, nodding his approval of "voluntary effort", encouraging the "citizen's sense of responsibility", recognising the rights of the individual to sue his representatives, and of his representatives who are dismissed from his service for suspected heresies, to demand to know of which heresies they are suspected of being guilty. But Big Brother will plan the economy ("we maintain that it is necessary for a Government consciously to plan the economic system"); Big Brother will abolish class-distinction in education and social welfare; and ultimately will decide that while all men are equal, some are more equal than others. For "it is right that special ability and industry, including thrift, inventiveness and excellence in the arts should be specially rewarded; but such recognition should be on merit alone and should not be allowed to lead to a new privileged class."

Having declared that Labour's three tasks are: "To transform the capitalist order into a socialist community" (it should be noted that this point is nowhere enlarged on in the pamphlet, so that the term

*One cannot help referring to the Collectivisation Decree in Catalonia during the Spanish Revolution (1936-39). This apparent legal regognition of the achievements of the social revolution far from assisting its "practical operation" hindered it to the point of ultimately destroying it, principally because, step by step, initiative and authority were transferred from the members of each collective to the government of Catalonia. And the government, which laid claim to being the expression of the social revolution (a claim based on the fact that all the workers' organisations were "represented" in it), eventually succeeded in even freeing itself of its revolutionary representation.

"socialist community" remains *vague* though it sounds *good*); "defend the advances we have already made; carry out our responsibilities within the existing system" — we are then told: "Rights mean duties. No one who benefits from the Welfare State, from full employment or from better education can contract out of the social obligations which must support these reforms."

If we are right in interpreting the reference to "social obligations" to mean that we must be behind the government — that is, respond to its calls for more production, more sacrifices to provide defence against those enemies who would wish to destroy our Welfare State, our way of life, etc. — then the statement is a dangerous one as well as being sheer hypocrisy.

It is sheer hypocrisy because here we have these self-styled socialists implying that social services, a job and a decent education, are *privileges* for which we should show ourselves grateful to the munificent government that bestows them on us (paying for them out of their own pockets).

It is dangerous because by using these arguments it means that in countries such as Russia, where the State controls everything, the citizen should therefore have even greater social obligations to the government and the system. At the other extreme, the worker, whose loaf of bread and the roof over his head depend on his earning a wage, has a very great social obligation to his employer. It means too that however close one may approximate to the "equalitarian society" economically and to "equality before the law", the social structure of government and State remains, and, if anything, is strenghthened, since it will control those private or monopolistic enterprises which to-day wield too much power for the liking of the Labour Party.

The producer, the employee, until he has direct control of his work; the consumer, until he determines what he needs (and this includes education, health services and other social services no less than the food he actually consumes); until that control begins at local level there can be no ethical argument to support this Labour Party idea of "duties", of "social obligations" or of condemnation of those who "contract out" whilst at the same time making use of the "benefits" of the Welfare State.

"Rights mean duties" is an authoritarian concept. Indeed, in the society of *real* personal freedom, the word "rights" would have no meaning for there would be no class nor political hierarchy with the power to impose its wishes on the individual or to grant him "rights" (generally in exchange for new duties).

The Welfare State, State education for everyone without class distinction, State control of production, are all roads which may lead to less inequality but inevitably lead to more State control; never to individual freedom. However, to seek to destroy them by armed revolution without at the same time having something to put in their place is to condemn society to death by starvation and disease. The organisation of production, distribution and the social and health services is vital to life, and cannot be suspended even for one moment. Why then, we may be asked, do we criticise the social democrats, the reformists and the gradualists who are, so they say, carrying on a "quiet revolution" through parliament, the trade unions and other organisations? The answer, as we see it, is that the Machine they seek to modify or to perfect is basically authoritarian, and just as you cannot make a silk purse out of a sow's ear, so is it impossible ever to build the free society with an organisation which is authoritarian.

If socialists and anarchists not only desire the free society but are also prepared to work for its attainment there are certain steps to be taken which, to our minds, cannot be by-passed even by the most impatient among us. The first is to influence and inspire our fellow-beings with a spirit of freedom (no mean task when one considers that, in fact, the whole Labour movement is vitiated by authoritarian ideas). Until the idea of freedom is felt strongly enough by a large minority it will be impossible to put into effect the second step, which must consist in creating our own organisations of self-help, our own local health services, our own schools, our own producers and consumers co-operatives. That is, instead of, as the Labour Party proposes, strengthening the State by ever extending its functions, we must withdraw initiative from the State and take it ourselves as responsible individuals and as members of communities with common needs and common problems.

We do not suggest that as a result of such steps the State will "wither away"; on the contrary it will probably use every means, foul or fair, to retain its power. What is certain, however, is that if and when the clash comes, it will not be because of a purely negative "discontent", which in the past has always resulted in a change of masters, but will truly represent *a struggle between two diametrically opposed ways of life:* the one based on freedom and voluntary co-operation, the other on authority, privilege and class distinctions.

But without individual effort, the willingness to accept the consequences of one's ideas wherever they lead, there can be no change. There is nothing inevitable about history. To coin the Labour Party's aphorism quoted earlier: Man makes history and not history Man! It is not enough to possess the idea, the seed of freedom. One must also sow it to reap the harvest.

[July 14, 1956]

EQUALITY THROUGH TAXATION?

The third of the Labour Party's pamphlets to appear deals with "social justice" and is given the title "Towards Equality". And just as their policy pamphlet on "Personal Freedom" told us very little about freedom and a great deal about how the Labour Party would operate the State machine for the good of the community, so their pamphlet on equality is a somewhat nebulous statement of how they propose to run the capitalist financial machine to ensure fair shares all round, revealing, in the process, that equality is much more a vote-catching slogan than a strongly-felt principle.

The Party's policy-makers in dealing with the subject of *equality* follow the same reasoning as they did earlier on the subject of *personal freedom* in that they are simply interested in sharing out the cake more equitably, but appear to be quite uninterested in the ingredients that go to make it or even how it has been made.

Thus when the subject under discussion was personal freedom they spent their time talking about Rights: the rights of the individual to sue the Crown and its agencies; the rights of everyone to have a job, or to share in those privileges which to-day were reserved for a minority of the community. There was no questioning the possibility that the real obstacle to personal freedom was the very structure of our present social organisation. Now, in their statement on Equality (true it's "*Towards* Equality" that the Labour Party have directed their unimaginative minds, though, as we hope to show, it leads to inequality) there is a certain realism in the introduction in which they declare:

> It would be foolish to assume that our objectives will be automatically achieved or that the injustices that still exist are no more than decaying relics of a bygone age. The truth is that there exists in a capitalist system a strong, persistent trend towards economic and social inequality.

But not only do they believe that this trend "can only be contained by deliberate and continuous State intervention"; they also (in the second part of their statement) make it quite clear that the classless, equalitarian society can function in a capitalist economy simply by applying certain financial curbs. In other words, they do not question the basic structure of the money and property-owning system but suggest that a financial curettage is all that is needed to remove the social injustices (which are outlined in Part One).

> The remedies . . . lie firstly in making present taxes really effective; secondly, and even more important, in correcting the present unequal distribution of private wealth and the tendency for it to accumulate in too few hands (p. 22).

Now let us, for a moment, examine the validity of the idea. In the introduction we are told:

> Fifty years ago the Labour Party brought to British politics a new and radical purpose. It determined to use the machinery of Parliamentary government not just to 'run the country' but to change the nature of society itself. Against the power of privilege and wealth, and the values of a capitalist society, it set the ideals of democratic socialism.
>
> It proclaimed the need for a new and classless society based upon equal chances for the nation's youth, regardless of birth, sex and fortune; a fair division and a planned expansion of the nation's wealth; the right to work; the elimination of poverty; common ownership, control or dispersal of economic power; service, not greed, as the driving social purpose.
>
> To-day, these are no longer the aims of a small band of Socialist pioneers, but the conscious ideals of more than half the nation. Certainly much progress has been made. The reforms of the 1945-51 Labour Government, following the vast upheavals of war, had opened a new and better era in our national life. The Welfare State which we then created is an achievement of which Labour feels justly proud.

It is admitted nevertheless that we are far from the equalitarian State; privilege remains "strongly entrenched" and the division of the "nation's wealth is still arbitrary and unjust". And in essentials "ours is — and is felt to be — a class society".

To our minds it is sheer distortion of the facts to attribute the undoubted improvement in living conditions in this country to six years of Labour "rule", and far from "feeling proud" at the results, they should admit that so far as governments go they have proved that no fundamental changes are ever brought about through government. The Labour Party recognises this fact, without however admitting it, when it enumerates the gross inequality in education ("A major cause of inequality in British society is our educational system"), in work ("The treatment of employees at work has always been, and still is, one of the most potent sources of inequality in our society"), in incomes, power and wealth.

How far six years of Labour rule succeeded in leading us towards equality can be gauged from the following admission:

> Half the nation own little more than their personal and household effects; one percent. of the nation own something like half the nation's private wealth. Even this contrast does not fully illustrate the continuing concentration of wealth. Here is another illustration: a quarter of the nation's private wealth consists of large fortunes of £50,000 and over — and these are owned by one fifth of one per cent. of the nation.

The Labour Party assumed the reins of government at a moment more than favourable for far-reaching changes in the economic and social structure of the country. Almost every country in the world emerged from the war in a radical mood. (Social democracy has little cause for self-congratulation on this score — for without them perhaps there would have been more of the *revolutionary* ferment that marked the last phases of the 1914-18 war).

In this country, Labour was swept into office as a result of the promises of pie-in-the-sky offered by Churchill (as the reward for more "blood, sweat and tears") which the workers and certain sections of the professional classes thought stood more chance of being implemented by Labour than by the Tories.

To say, however, that the Welfare State and Full Employment are "achievements" of Labour rule is sheer nonsense.

> In spite of the great post-war extension of the social services, we have no reason to be complacent. The Welfare State has not, as some have optimistically claimed, abolished poverty everywhere — although it has greatly reduced what was, in the inter-war period, its most important and conspicuous cause: namely, unemployment.

Full employment and prosperity have nothing to do with the Welfare State, and a great deal to do with a world at peace but on a war footing. Indeed, there is more general prosperity in free-for-all America than in this Welfare State of ours. And can any Labour policy-maker deny that without the vast armament programme and millions of potential producers uselessly absorbed in the armed forces, productive capacity would have long ago outstripped "demand" (not needs) and the "redundancy" which is making itself felt at present in the car industry would have long ago affected industry as a whole? If the Labour Party were in power, what measures would they take to guarantee full employment, without lowering workers' living standards, or increasing expenditure on armaments?

Their policy statement does not reveal any secret of how to square the (vicious) circle of capitalist economics. We suspect that their silence is a confession of their impotence.

The Labour thinkers have an unoriginal concept of equality. If one understands them correctly they favour only *equality of opportunity*.

> The point we wish to emphasise is not that competitive examinations are unfair, but the different types of schools are bound to give very unequal chances of success. (p. 7).

And a few pages later, on the subject of Equality and Income, they conclude that "provided there is a decent minimum wage" they see no objection to a system of rewards which is related to the nature and difficulty of the work, the skills required and the responsibility borne.

> Differences in earned income, based on these tests, makes sense. How wide the gap should eventually be between top and bottom, floor and ceiling, is something which cannot be decided in the abstract. Much depends upon the climate of opinion, upon what each generation is accustomed to and what it therefore expects.

It seems quite clear to us that what the Labour Party are out to achieve is the equal opportunity for all, irrespective of their social or economic background, to obtain key jobs in the political and industrial fields, that is, to become members of the ruling hierarchy. It is significant that these ardent advocates of the "classless society" should place so much importance on the "professions, the State service and managerial and technical posts" . . . and on the "highly competitive examinations for entrance to the Foreign Service and to the Administrative Class of the Home Civil Service". The fact that these posts may one day be open to the sons of humble workers as well as the sons of the "upper classes" will not mean the end of the class system. The class structure will remain. At most a limited number of persons will feel that they have changed their status, their class.

In the final analysis class consciousness is a feeling of inferiority — or superiority — and much less a question of one's income or the "importance" of one's job, though of course it can be argued that these are the values that create the feelings of inferiority and superiority. Exactly. But only so long as we are stupid enough to accept these values!

The Labour Party recognise this when they refer to the shabby treatment of employees which, they point out, is not "simply a question of the range of income and salaries . . . but also of the treatment and consideration shown to different classes of employees". But instead of stressing that all work which contributes to the welfare of the community is valuable, they betray their class consciousness by dealing at great length with the question of workers having opportunities for "rising" to executive posts. Which is not surprising when one considers that the Trade Union movement is as class-ridden as the society on whose survival its own survival depends, and that its leaders are offered, and invariably accept, the "honours" which are the very symbol of that class-society.

Equality will not come about by legislation or by some cunning financial sleight of hand by the Labour Party economists. In the first place we need to agree what is meant by equality, and if it means what we think it means, then the Labour Party will have to do a lot more re-thinking than it has done so far. But what is more important, the victims of our unequal society must start thinking for themselves. We are sure it will help them to lose their feeling of inferiority and their fatalism.

[July 28, 1956]

CAPITALISM IN SHEEP'S CLOTHING?

It is difficult to say whether the high spirits in which both the Labour and Tory Party conferences concluded their deliberations were due to a closing of the ranks, the discovery of "real unity", and a "deep sense of purpose" among the respective delegates, or just simply that the air both in Scarborough and Blackpool is so bracing that even cliché-worn politicians and flat-footed Trade Union leaders, after a few days by the sea, can rise to the occasion. For all they did was to repeat the same old slogans but with just that extra bit of enthusiasm, which the ozonised delegates present were quick to sense, as was demonstrated by the indiscriminate applause with which each wave of verbiage was received. (At the Tory conference even the Stewards carried out their duties as "chuckers-out" with more zeal than even the Prime Minister thought necessary.)

But seriously, the Labour Party conference was principally concerned with the problem of how to win the next elections, and all discussion which attempted to recall Conference to *principles* was stifled by the platform along which were ranged the ageing shadow government desperately seeking to placate the "middle class" whose votes they need if they are to taste the sweet fruits of office before senility or the limbo of the House of Lords sweeps them from the political scene.

The Tories, on the other hand, are in power, and their leader, who makes his dramatic appearance only at the end of the Conference to do the talking and not the listening, has been "meeting the people", has been giving Eisenhower and Dulles sound advice over "Red China", has reduced the Bank rate and increased the dollar reserves, and is sitting pretty, according to the public opinion polls. The Tory conference was concerned not with winning the next election but with retaining power. And being sporting people addressing a sporting public the outstanding slogan of the Tory conference, uttered by the greatest publicist of them all, Lord Hailsham, was "Operation Hat-Trick". This combined military-sporting action would in Lord Hailsham's view not only mean that there would be another Conservative Government but "The evil, fatuous spectre of democratic Socialism, that contradiction in terms", would disappear "into the mists of time. We shall have taken the robber castle," he went on, "torn down its battlements, stormed its keep, and liberated its dungeons."

The only objection any sincere Socialist could have to Hailsham's outburst is that he is really much too flattering. For years the Labour Party leadership has been adding so much water to its already much watered socialism that some defeatist socialists declare that they cannot taste the wine for the water. (But equally there are true-blue Tories who declare that the Tory Port of the good old days has been ousted by these upstarts whose political palates have been destroyed by port-type wines. These Tory idealists are regularly and unceremoniously ejected at "Tory" gatherings, just as the Socialist idealists are shouted down at theirs or expelled from the Party.)

And, of course, it is true that during the past fifteen years the "ideological" gap between the two major political parties has been bridged: by the Labourites throwing overboard the ideological content of their programme, and by the Conservatives seeking an ideology which had a more popular appeal in an era of universal suffrage. At a time when the Labour Party is soft-pedalling the principle of nationalisation*, and so qualifying the concept of "equality" that it has lost all meaning, the Conservative Party is, on paper at least, falling over backwards to disown the traditional Capitalist, and seeking to pose as the champion of the People *versus* the State.

The publication of the booklet "Prospect for Capitalism" is an attempt by the Conservative Party to present Capitalism not as a swear word (for the Left) but as an economic system which takes into account the aspirations and ambitions of a majority of the population and which therefore will, if not misrepresented, appeal to a majority of the people. Similarly, the various Labour Party policy pamphlets — and in particular the one, "Towards Equality" — were the Labour Party's attempt to reassure the professional, the middle-class of this country, that their brand of "socialism" had nothing to do with Marx, was not revolutionary, and only believed in "equality" to the extent that 'some are more equal than others'. And, far from discouraging "initiative", considered that "provided there is a decent minimum wage" they had no objection to a system of rewards which is related to the nature and difficulty of the work, the skills required and the responsibility borne. Which is what Lord Hailsham says in his foreword to "Prospect for Capitalism":

> Capital became unpopular not because it failed but in the measure in which it succeeded. The demand that its benefits should be more widely shared, and that the freedom from restriction should not be allowed to develop into abuse of human dignity, became irresistible. The evangelical fervour of philanthropists like Lord Shaftesbury, and the political nous of statesmen like Lord Beaconsfield taught us the overriding necessity to discipline business oligarchies and profit motives with those traditions of service, obligation, and charity which had once tempered the rule of a landed aristocracy.

*On the other hand, Lord Hailsham refers to the emergence of technical limitations on the development of capitalism which are more serious than the Marxian analysis: activities whose economic advantages or disadvantages cannot be measured in terms of their immediate profitability. He mentions the cost of cleansing the air and water, and road development, as examples. Can one expect Lord Hailsham to come forward soon as an advocate of a limited nationalisation?

But the people of this country must be wary of these attempts to dress up wolves in sheep's clothing, however ridiculous Hailsham may appear when he makes an exhibition of himself or however convincing Macmillan may seem when he turns on his best bedside or fireside manner. Capitalism, according to our dictionary, is "the system that favours the concentration of capital in the hands of the few". Bearing in mind this definition, the following from Hailsham's foreword has a cynical ring about it:

> It will indeed be the test of conservatism in the coming generation that it should not only create the property-owning democracy but should temper the materialism and acquisitive spirit of the many with a sense of service and responsibility, as once it tempered the excesses of the early capitalists and so confounded Marx.

In other words he wants the people to feel they have a stake in the capitalist society by owning their own back yard, but he does not want them to be much more ambitious than that even though the resolution following the debate on Industrial Relations "reaffirms" the Conservative Party's belief in "a partnership between Government, employers and workers" and many of the delegates talked in specific terms of workers as shareholders in industry.

The fact of workers owning their houses and investing their savings in shares in Industry will not change their situation of inferiority in existing society. On the contrary, if anything it will consolidate it. As the *Manchester Guardian* financial column put it: "the more people with a monetary interest in the present system the less likely is the system to be disturbed by a Labour Government" (it being assumed that Labour is synonymous with revolution and change). Capitalism cannot be reformed. If one believes in the capitalist system one believes in all those privileges which the socialists and the anarchists, of the 19th century, condemned without ifs and buts as offensive to the elementary dignity of the working man. Many of the rough edges of capitalism have been knocked off, not as a result of capitalists having a conscience but through agitation by their victims. Yet the main structure remains intact, preserved not only by the Hailshams, but by the Gaitskells and the Bevans, whatever they may say at party conferences.

[October 18, 1958]

PROSPERITY — ON PAPER

The Labour Party's Election Manifesto presented in the form of a "Personal Guide to The Future Labour Offers YOU" is a slick production with cellophaned cover (impervious to sullying by workers' grubby hands) and neatly thumb-indexed for quick reference (which will surely appeal to white collar workers accustomed to ledgers and address books, or who are daily irritated at having to wade through badly indexed volumes of rules and regulations). Furthermore, what must have accounted for the huge sales of this Guide (650,000 copies sold in the first fortnight) is that it offers a bargain-happy public something for nothing — or very nearly. For six coppers one is offered a brochure which has probably cost three times that amount to produce. But to our minds the price of the brochure was determined less by considerations of mass circulation than by creating just this impression of offering the public something for nothing: for sixpence you have a pamphlet "outlining the plans which the next Labour Government will turn into reality" declares a smiling Hugh Gaitskell on the first page; and to get that Labour government which is going to do so much for you, all you have to do is to make sure to put your cross against the name of the Labour candidate at the next general election!

For that cross the Labour Party offers you full employment, a home of your own (with bathroom and kitchen), "first-rate" education for your children, more hospitals, more nurses, free chiropody (for the aged) and free drugs. For that cross for Labour you will be protected from hire-purchase ramps and will get value for your money; your children will get a good start in life (careers and culture for everybody), and the old folk will be so happy they won't want to die. Public control of industry and finance will solve the problem of unemployment and small farmers will be cared for by Big Brother. Under Labour, Taxes will go down (except for the "spivs and the stock exchange gamblers") and the prospect of Peace will go up (nevertheless "Labour fully accepts the duty of maintaining the military defences of Britain"). The future of the Commonwealth and the Colonies, presented in four colours, is almost too good to be true: "fair shares for the hungry people of the world", protection of the African majorities, encouragement of the growth of co-operatives and trade unions, and one percent. of the national income for raising the standard of living in these territories.

These are the thumb-nail bargains in the Labour Party basement all at a cost of sixpence *and* (it is a very important "and") your cross for the Labour candidate when the time comes. But we have not come to the end of the Guide. A light green arrow directs us to turn the page to "and now the Future" where . . . no, it's not Old Moore himself waiting for us, nor even a picture of the milky way. A double page photograph of a view across a lake, loch or, perhaps, an artificial reservoir under which some charming village is buried, is lighted up in one corner by a shaft of sunlight which has penetrated a beautiful but nevertheless ominously clouded sky. The text which follows makes it clear that it won't rain — indeed it will be a permanently blue sky — if Mr. Gaitskell and his friends run the government. The plans are no "blueprint for Utopia" but what *can* be done (their italics) in "the next five years of Labour Government". Theirs is "a *practical* assessment of the jobs to be done, and a *realistic* account of the way we propose to do it".

But in fairness to the boys of Transport House, under their practical black three-piece suits and watch chains beat hearts not of gold but full of socialism and brotherly love.

A political programme is not just a statement of intentions. It also expresses an attitude to life.

We in the Labour Party are Socialists. This means that our whole approach to politics is different from that of the Tories. What is the difference?

Whereas the Tories believe that the "major economic and political decisions should be taken by the rich and powerful — government by 'top people' ", Labour's approach is based on two Socialist ideals: "Mutual service — the story of the Good Samaritan in terms of everyday political life" and "the enlargement of personal freedom" for others as well as for oneself. "There can be no true freedom without social justice".

These Socialist ideals have shaped our present programme. We express our ideals, first of all, in the material care of those who most need it . . .

We know that true happiness does not come from material prosperity. (But poverty causes an immense amount of human *un*happiness). Happiness comes from a full, free, satisfying life — a decent home, a secure job that you like doing, leisure richly filled with the good things of civilisation.

But all this must be "planned" and "fought for by all those who understand the modern world better than the Tories do", and who have "seen the vision of a just society and are inspired by the purpose of helping to create it".

It is they who have *sustained* the Labour Party in the battle against war and want and ignorance. We believe that the British people will soon decide to take, *with Labour,* another great step in the exciting future. (Our italics)

So, fellow worker, ladies and gentlemen, "sustain" the Labour Party and see the new world in glorious technicolour. Price sixpence and your cross!

The Future Labour Offers You is too slick both in its presentation and its content to be Socialist or true. The production, left to the professional publicity boys, is in the most expensive traditions of proprietary medicine advertising, suitable for selling pills and panaceas but not socialism; the content, cooked up by the successful journalist-intellectual-economist bright boys of the Party, aims at the lowest common denominator both in human intelligence and petty materialism. We quoted at length the "idealistic" passages in the brochure in the interests of fair reporting, not because we believe them when they say "we in the Labour Party are Socialists" or that they believe in socialism ("democratic socialism in action" is how Gaitskell describes the plan). The Labour Party hierarchy is out to win the sweet fruits of office; for this they need votes. Hence they offer a plan which aims at pandering to the material interests of a majority of the population — but, then, so do the Tories, and, so far, quite successfully.

Obviously, Labour have two trump cards in their pack: the Rent Act and unemployment. A decent roof over your heads is a must in the Labour plan. It will "encourage" home ownership. Like their Tory rivals these "socialists" want to see a "property-owning democracy" in action. But they will repeal the Rent Act which decontrolled 800,000 rented houses. The Act they will put in its place will restore security of tenure to these houses, stop further decontrol and ensure "fair rents for both furnished and unfurnished lettings by setting up Rent Tribunals".

Second to *Your Home* in this thumb index socialism is *Your Job.* "You" are shown lustily wielding a shovel and are reminded that

The great ideal of Jobs For All first became a peace-time reality under the 1945 Labour Government. Under the Tories fear of the sack has returned.

The first objective of the Labour Government will be to *restore* full employment and to *preserve* full employment. This is the prime purpose of our plan for controlled expansion.

It is true that "fear of the sack" has returned under the Tories, but if the Labour Party takes credit for full employment in the "peace years" 1945-1951* then the Tories are equally justified in patting themselves on the back for maintaining full employment between 1951 and 1957. There is not a scrap of evidence to show that the Labour Party has the answer to unemployment. Full employment in Britain during the post-war years 1945-57 was maintained under Labour and Tory governments because world markets, *thanks to the devastation of six years of war,* could absorb, and pay for in cash or raw materials, more than the industrial nations could produce. Even 'old-fashioned' Tories believe in full employment when there is a sellers' market. It is only when markets shrink and price, not availability, decides where orders will go, that the Tory wolf removes his sheep's clothing and looks to unemployment as the incentive for increased productivity (not production**). What do the Labour Party offer as an alterantive? It is quite simple, and most revealing.

The Labour Party's Plan for better this and more of that, of a sprightly Age and a carefree (but career-minded) Youth — all this depends on "our success in achieving year by year a rapid expansion of production". This is how it all works in the "Socialists' " capitalist paradise.

The Tories declare that the nation cannot afford Labour's social programme without "crushing increases in the burden of taxes"; Labour replies by reminding the Tories that if industrial production in the past three years had gone up "as fast as it did under the Labour Government" our national income to-day would be £1,700 million higher and the Chancellor of the Exchequer "would be collecting £450 million more revenue without adding a farthing to existing tax rates". Note the cunningness of the argument.

So first, Labour "will end Tory restrictions on production" and it will be "Full-capacity" for machines, factories and workers. Secondly, a plan for capital investment "which will put more horsepower at the elbow of workers in industry and in agriculture", for "to survive in the world's markets we *must* increase productivity per man", which is, of course, what the Tories are also saying. The fact that the Labour

*In 1951 under the "peace-time" Labour government an armaments programme of £4,700 millions was announced which Mr. Gaitskell, then Chancellor of the Exchequer, told the Commons would necessitate "some local interference with house building in the interests of defence work". He was announcing cuts of at least £100 million in buildings and in equipment for industry.

**Only last week the President of the British Employers' Confederation at a glass manufactuerers' lunch referred to the unemployment figures and said it was important that the Government "should not re-create the acute shortage of skilled labour which has so long bedevilled our efforts to increase efficiency".

plan states that increased productivity comes from increased horse-power — as well as from higher managerial efficiency, improved planning, more and better scientific research but makes no reference to more efficient workers as well, is probably just an electoral over-sight which will be put right if and when they have got all the votes they need to win the elections.

Assuming that the Labour plan is operating thus far*, and the miners are producing more coal than ever, while thousands of labourers are shovelling the £70 millions worth of Tory coal dumped in quarries during the wicked '50s into trucks for the steelworks which under "Tory stagnation" were only working to 80 per cent. capacity ("Steel" is described as "the thermometer of a nation's health. Would the nation's life-blood be the automobile, perchance?) and industry in general was humming away night and day, horse-powers and elbows combining in happy Socialist emulation, what are we supposed to do with all the goods we produce?

As we write we are feverishly thumbing our way down the *Future Labour Offer You* to find the official answer, but there is none. We have found the following, however: "No wonder Britain (as a result of Tory policy) is falling behind her competitors — Germany, Japan, Russia — in the world race for higher production."

Do we conclude from this that full employment and all the tantalising tit-bits so tastefully offered by Transport House in their "Personal Guide" depend, after all, on ousting our "competitors" in the "world race" for . . . markets?

Apart from the fact that Britain's best markets are among her competitors and potential competitors who, if she filches their markets, will have less to spend on imports, it has always been the race for markets which in the past has also invariably led to war which, the Guide, if thumbed at "Peace", tells us Labour will take active steps to abolish from the face of the earth.

Even assuming that such a policy does not lead to war, it means that Labour proposes to achieve its economic objectives at the expense of workers in the competing industrial nations. And where does their "first socialist ideal (of) mutual service — the story of the Good Samaritan in terms of everyday political life", come in?

*We omitted to add the third prong of the Labour plan for prosperity: "Labour is pledged to maintain the value of the pound and to keep Britain the financial centre of the Commonwealth and the Sterling area". Which is what Mr. Amory declared recently and what poor Mr. Thorneycroft said before him. Probably Mr. Gaitskell said that too way back in 1951 when he was Chancellor.

The answer, without calling for more documentary evidence, is that it doesn't. Capitalism is a system based on privilege and just as it benefits a few at the expense of the many within a nation, so can it serve to benefit the people of a few nations at the expense of the people of many other nations.

It is not by chance, nor for biological reasons, that more than half the world's people still live in a state of starvation and ignorance. It is not by chance that as the living standards in the have-countries rise, so those of the have-not countries are relatively, and in some cases actually, depressed.

Labour's plan for prosperity and full employment is capitalist and not socialist, and cannot work except at the expense of the living standards of workers in other industrial countries. It won't work even then because every industrial nation in the world is using similar means to achieve better or worse ends.

The Labour Party's is a feeble, outworn and unimaginative attempt to curb "the excess" of private capitalism by further increasing the power and functions of the State. This road leads neither to Socialism nor to the abolition of the social injustices which are at the root of Capitalism. It simply creates new injustices, and leads to an even greater concentration of power.

[December 13, 1958]

SECURITY MINDEDNESS

The dominating feature of the Labour Party's "Personal Guide to the Future Labour Offers You" is *Security* from the womb to the tomb. With homes and jobs for everyone and education and careers irrespective of class and financial distinctions; a future for youth, and an old-age without fear: value for money (by smashing the monopolies and keeping the pound sterling "strong") and a healthy people irrespective of costs; and last, but not least, defending us, with H-bombs if necessary, from any would-be aggressor, the Labour Party is offering just what Mass Man craves for most: Security.

Mr. Macmillan too offers the British people security in return for their votes. Only last week-end in Newcastle-upon-Tyne he was pointing out that what Labour was only promising in some possible future, the Tories were actually providing in the present: more houses, more schools and smaller classes, less taxes and higher pensions. BUT

> Of course, in an economy as delicately balanced as ours there is bound to be some fluctuation. There are bound to be, as the techniques and industries change, difficulties in this or that locality (but all this can be easily managed) so long as we do not let events take charge of us but remain in charge of them.

This passing reference to our delicately balanced economy is a polite way of saying that however much the government-of-the-day might wish to ensure full employment and prosperity for all, security for all, the fact remains that for one reason or another some will always be more secure than others, some will have to join the dole queues, some young people will leave school only to sign on at the labour exchange, some old people will have to expect eviction from their homes or be expected to live on less than the minimum...

The security-mindedness of people in the Western world, which gives rise to the growing incidence of mental diseases associated with anxiety and insecurity, is we think the direct result of a social organisation based on centralised government, and of production and distribution based on profit and not needs. We believe that Man at all times in his history has sought security (if only because he has survived to this day, or rather, has managed to survive when the "forces of nature" coupled with Man's lack of knowledge of himself and his surroundings made survival an end in itself). But unless we make a clear distinction between the security-mindedness of modern industrial man (which generally leads either to a smug, self-satisfied but amorphous conformism, or to the mental hospitals) and the struggles of our ancestors, some of the backward peoples in the world to-day, and even the struggling revolutionary minorities in our own time . . . we were saying, unless we make a clear distinction, we shall never understand the causes of the neuroses in this age of potential prosperity and material security.

Perhaps we can make this distinction clearer by a simple analogy. Put two experienced drivers in a car, one in the driving seat, the other as a passenger by his side. Though they both desire the same ends — that is they want to get to say Brighton — the driver-driver arrives at their destination fresh and cheerful, whereas the driver-passenger is worn out, his right leg stiff with having applied brakes-that-were-not-there all along the route! In other words, just as a driver feels really secure only when he is driving, so does Man only feel really secure when he actually controls his means of life, or is free to seek those means.

The primitive hunter in most cases has a more precarious existence than a factory worker, yet because survival largely depends on his resources and initiative, whereas the factory worker is at the mercy of fashion (the Joneses as determined by the Advertisers), competition, world markets and unemployment — that is, factors outside his control — the anxiety or feeling of insecurity which both may experience *are not of the same order.* The factory worker has no control over his job or the financial mincing machine from which his daily stint emerges as bread, bread and butter or bread and margarine. His insecurity and anxiety are based on a feeling of impotence, of dependence on the "generosity" or willingness of others to provide him with the essentials of life. The primitive hunter, on the other hand, is not only in complete command of his skill, experience and strength but also in direct contact with the sources of his sustenance. For him failure to survive is a matter accountable to natural causes or his own shortcomings as a hunter. For the factory worker unemployment, slums, relief, domestic strife and emptiness are the hazards of birth which only a philanthropic government or Mr. Littlewoods' penny-pools may or may not relieve.

It is unnecessary to point out that we do not think the alternative to an existence as a factory worker, and all that is involved, psychologically and physically, in this *condition ouvriere* is a world of primitive hunters! What we *are* saying, however, is that the almost pathological concern to-day with security and, in consequence, the general refusal to consider, on their merits, as ways of life, those ideas such as Anarchism which seek to relate the intuitive desire for survival to a *joie de vivre,* is based on a fundamental misunderstanding of society as it is to-day and of the needs of ordinary human beings. Admitted Man's striving after some kind of security; a security which once it exists makes life a means to an end instead of the end. But the world in which we live denies that right, for it raises the nation, the State, the social and economic organisation above the individual. Capitalism is, by definition, a system which operates in the material interests of a minority of the community; power politics satisfies the unhealthy desires of a very small number of people in the world as well as providing comfortable jobs for many more; the division of the world into nations serves no *useful* purpose, except for those individuals whose livelihood and privileges depend on such a division, from the modest customs officials to the exalted ambassadors (with their £6,000 per annum salaries plus £24,000 per annum expenses), from the underpaid flag-spangled interpreters to the suave arm-chaired directors of national culture in foreign lands.

The application of modern science to transportation has shrunk the world of Mozart's day into a mere Austria, yet more insularity exists to-day than ever before. We know, a matter of hours after its occurrence, what diabolical tricks Nkrumah's government is up to in Ghana or the excesses Dr. Castro's followers are indulging in in Cuba; we know when Russia tests an H-bomb (whether they release the news or not) or when the British torture a Cypriot, but generally not only do our protests not reach the people of the countries concerned, but when they do, the popular reaction is the contrary of what one would expect . . . simply because the growth of communications, far from encouraging a world outlook, has lowered the iron curtains between nations — and fomented nationalistic pride* which is both irrational and hysterical.

For us it is significant that the *Oxford Concise Dictionary* gives as its first definition of security, "over-confidence". As anarchists we welcome the definition because we enjoy the insecurity, the adventure, the "unknown" in life. But Mr. Fowler and his later editors must have had a shrewd understanding of things as they are when they refused to follow other lexicographers who defined security as "the state or condition of being secure . . . freedom from danger or risk . . . freedom from care or apprehension**. For this,

*As travel becomes, physically speaking, easier, so bureaucratic barriers become more difficult! Fifty years ago a "foreigner" coming to Britain required no passport. To-day he requires a passport, perhaps a visa, invariably he needs to complete a form *and* satisfy an immigration officer that he is a *bona fide* visitor or a rich-, professional-man's servant.

**Funk & Thomas, 1922.

indeed, is Utopia! In the best of worlds "danger and risk" cannot be excluded; in a capitalist world there is no "condition of being secure", if only because the capitalist world is a world divided, in which the "interests" of one section of the community more often than not can only be satisfied at the expense of the interests of the other.

For example: most people would feel more secure if production of nuclear weapons were stopped. Yet many workers are earning large wages producing these armaments and resent interference from those who would deprive them of a job. Most people would welcome the extension of smokeless zones in the big cities of the world. This means dispensing with coal for domestic purposes. Miners, on the other hand, are urging their governments to encourage the use of coal in increasing quantities in order to prevent unemployment in the coal industry. The government proposes to effect drastic economies in the navy; workers in naval ship yards and docks, as well as admirals, protest at the proposed cuts. There is a crisis now in the bicycle industry. For nine months Raleigh Industries Ltd. have been working a four day week; now 500 out of the factory's 7,000 workers are being sacked. To solve their problem fewer people should be buying motor-cycles and cars. But in solving their problems more people would be put out of work in the car and motor-cycle industries.

Even in Switzerland workers in the watch industry are not allowed to feel any sense of security. Price competition from Germany, tariff barriers in America and a new watch industry in India have made the Swiss workers aware of the fact that they can be sure of nothing (for the first time in living memory Swiss watchmakers are out of work), and Swiss watch manufacturers that tradition has no place in a world of competition (after all, why should they have a monopoly in watches any more than the French in champagne or the Scots in whisky?).

Yes, the world we live in is worse than the jungle for we neither use our intelligence nor have the instincts to further the survival of our species. Every man lives in his own self-made little prison, resentful of his fate yet accepting to pay for the governments and the warders who put him, and keep him, there. And in prison the only security they are interested in is the one which ensures that their prisoners shall not escape.

Anarchism, because it places the responsibility on the individual and not the guardians, at least puts one on the road to that minimum security to which, we believe, every individual born into this world, is entitled, yet without dulling the human personality into blind acceptance of authority. At most it informs those material needs with a philosophy of life along the elusive road of human happiness.

[January 24, 1959]

SIGNPOST TO NOWHERE

Signpost for the Sixties is a statement of Labour Party home policy to be submitted by the National Executive to the Annual Conference being held in Blackpool in October. In the words of the authors of the statement, they "have not tried to draw up a comprehensive manifesto". There is time between now and the next general election for the "situation to change" and "we would regard it as folly to anticipate at this Conference the Party's election programme". In a previous Party publication the general secretary, Mr. Morgan Phillips, had written, however, that

> What the party needs today is not another batch of policy documents or detailed blueprints but a clear statement both of our distinctive attitude to post-war capitalism and of the new direction we should give the nation's affairs.

With this view the authors of Signpost for the Sixties "concur", and they declare that their "single aim has been to make good (that) important deficiency in the formulation of Socialist policy". To this end they have

> highlighted five themes — planning and economic expansion, the use of our land, a new approach to social security, equality and educational opportunity and fair taxation. These issues, we believe, are becoming increasingly significant and they illustrate both our critique of the Tory Affluent Society and the Socialist remedies we recommend.

In spite of these two references in the Foreword to "Socialist policy" and "Socialist remedies" the pages that follow are as barren of socialism as they are of what Mr. Phillips referred to as a "distinctive attitude" to post-war capitalism or of "the new direction" he thought the party should give the nation's affairs. If one can describe *Signpost for the Sixties* in a sentence: it is an attempt to save capitalism in this country and "to prevent Britain from becoming a backwater" which, it is alleged, is our fate if our affairs remain in the hands of a Tory government and a handful of industrial monopolists.

We are told that "we live in a scientific revolution". That in the past fifteen years "man's knowledge and his power over nature" have grown more than in the previous century. It is "an epoch of revolutionary change". But far from concluding that the "scientific revolution" can only be matched by a revolution in our thinking, the Labour Party pundits because they cannot see beyond the tips of their noses, can only offer this kind of stuff:

> In such an epoch of revolutionary change, those who identify *laissez faire* with liberty are enemies, however unwitting, of democracy. The enlargement of freedom which we all desire cannot be achieved by opposing State intervention but only by assuring that national resources are wisely allocated and community services are humanely planned.

It should be unnecessary to state that anarchists are not opposed to planning. Whenever we write that production should be geared to satisfying human needs we are clearly expressing a belief that production (and services, of course) should be planned in the interests of the consumer, who is at the same time the producer. Such a planned economy, however, does not require centralised government, experts, executives or technocrats (however humane) determining for us what are our needs, *if the power lies with the people.* And it has to be pointed out, since most "socialists" seem to have forgotten, that this is what democracy is supposed to be all about. But the Labour Party "socialists" are not really concerned with the relationship between production and living, however much they may defend health services, education-for-all, housing for the people and security for the aged. Their statement is a long apologia for the capitalist system with large doses of State control to counteract the crises of capitalism.

> Our rate of industrial advance has been faltering; and the rapid and continuous expansion required to keep abreast of our competitors has been frustrated. Every time production has increased, we have run into an export-import crisis and industrial production has been halted once again by a credit squeeze and by other government restrictions.

The seriousness of these "crises" is not so much their effect on the ordinary people whose lives are not all that much upset by these "high-level economic problems", as the long-term effect on the nation as a nation.

Like any other great organisation, a nation that fails to make progress soon begins to slip backwards. In this epoch of change, to stand still is to decline. The danger that faces us, after a decade of complacent Tory Government is not the sudden catastrophe of slump and mass unemployment but piecemeal economic deterioration and gradual political decline. These processes of decay have, indeed, already begun. But there is still time to halt them and to restore that public spirit and collective dynamic which this country needs if it is to remain prosperous and to play its full role in the second half of the twentieth century.

It is difficult to know where to start commenting. It is clear that it is not only de Gaulle who dreams of a strong, influential *patrie;* for the language of the last two sentences we have quoted from the Gaitskell-Crossman document, only has meaning in such a context. Otherwise from a socialist point of view it is just a lot of balderdash. (Incidentally, they talk of "restoring" that public spirit, etc., but when did it exist before? Was there a time when the capitalists were jolly decent chaps? Or were they thinking of the bad — good? — old days when workers really did work and doffed their caps to the master and didn't keep on thinking about more wages and fewer working hours?).

But it is just as well, perhaps, to rid oneself of the illusion that the Labour Party "socialists" of the 2nd International are internationalists. If one accepts that they are chauvinists at heart it will be easier to explain their attitude to such questions as unilateralism in our time and to war at all times. And the Labour Party's document is full of revealing passages which illustrate the narrowness of their political and economic horizons.

For instance, in references to take-overs in which not only do firms swallow each other up but are "even swallowed up by foreign firms", and to private finance, the term "unpatriotic" is twice used:

The British people cannot be asked much longer to subscribe to this curious and fundamentally unpatriotic doctrine.

The fulfilment of the plan, therefore, must not be sacrificed to the dictates of private finance, of private profit or speculation, or outmoded financial techniques, or unpatriotic manoeuvrings in foreign exchange.

"In this epoch of change, to stand still is to decline." In the context in which the Labour Party refer to "change", that is changing techniques, new gimmicks, sales talk, etc., this is a myth, assuming we are talking in terms of people and not of business and finance. They lament the fact that our road system is "antiquated" but proudly point to "achievements" which are the result of State-subsidised research:

Jet aircraft would not have been produced without a massive investment of public money, or television without the joint enterprise of the Post Office and the B.B.C. The National Research Development Corporation, set up by the Labour Government, has sponsored the industrial development of scores of new inventions, among them the Hovercraft and advanced electronic brains and digital computers...

Are those of us who prefer the country lanes to the motorways, who have no inclination to travel by jet or cross the channel in a hovercraft, who haven't found time to look at TV and who prefer to use their own brains rather than an electronic brain to work out our problems... are we standing still, poor backwoodsmen in decline?

But of course these politicians are not thinking in terms of people but of the system, with the health of which, the Labour Party "socialists" are in certain respects more concerned than the *laissez faire* Tories. Their programme attempts to give more stability to the capitalist system — not to abolish it; they object to the present social discrimination in choosing the men at the top but not to the pyramid of power and privilege:

With certain honourable exceptions, our finance and industry need a major shake-up at the top. Too many Directors owe their position to family, school or political connections. If the dead wood were cut out of Britain's boardrooms and replaced by the keen young executives, production engineers and scientists, who are at present denied their legitimate prospects of promotion, our production and export problems would be much easier to solve.

Higher Education, under the Labour Party plan, must be available to all, for the good of the State.

Children are the nation's most valuable asset. What we spend on their schooling earns a bigger return in the quality of our national life than any other expenditure. This is more true than ever in the age of scientific revolution, when the improvement of our living standards and our survival as a free democracy depends upon the quality of our scientific, technological and technical education.

And whilst the shortage of places in establishments for higher education exists

we must be sure none of them are wasted; in particular, we must make sure that poor but able students are not excluded from universities by wealthier parents buying places for less-gifted children.

So under a Labour administration one would replace the privilege due to wealth by a privilege of brains. The injustice to the young people concerned, it seems to us, is as great under both systems, and it is only when one sees higher education as a vital aspect of the power- and/or economic-struggles that one can blithely advocate one injustice to replace another and pride oneself on being democratic.

The Labour Party's Orwellian concept that "all men are equal but some are more equal than others" emerges in the section dealing with *New Needs in Social Security.* The statement first complains that there are two standards of social security as a result of the various private welfare schemes which have been encouraged by the Tories through generous tax concessions to the firms concerned. They want to see this inequality abolished: "the privileges voluntarily conceded to some employees must now be transformed into the right of every citizen". So one of the first jobs of the "next" Labour Government will be

completely to recast the level of contributions and benefits in the Government's scheme, so as to achieve Labour's aim of ensuring that everyone gets at least half pay on retirement . . . in return for contributing a percentage of his wage or salary towards superannuation.

On the question of National Insurance the statement declares that

In the modern expanding economy, flat-rate contributions are out of date. They are a poll tax which lets the prosperous off lightly and imposes an unjust burden on the lower paid worker. We must now move forward, in the case of sickness as well as of old age pensions, to a new graduated system, *in which benefits are wage-regulated and contributions are paid as a percentage of earnings.* (Our italics.)

Again one injustice has been replaced by another. That the lower paid worker should contribute the same amount as the business executive to insurance schemes and draw the same benefits seemed unfair to the Labour Party socialists. To remedy this they propose a graduated contribution based on a workers' earnings so that the lower paid will contribute less than the highly paid. But when it comes to benefits these will be based on their *earnings* so that wage differentials which existed between them during their working lives will be applied in sickness and in old age. Is this socialism?

The Labour Party's plan for saving capitalism is a simple one. In the early stages of their "national plan" capital investment and exports would have to be given priority. "Economic growth" must be achieved without inflation. This demands "self-discipline" by the people, which, though they don't say so in so many words, means a curb on wage demands and on profits and tax evasion. So long as the people are "satisfied that both benefits and burdens are being fairly shared" they will show the self-discipline needed to restore the old country to its former glory.

We would be the last to deny that the Labour Party statement does contain factual material on the Land racket, on education, on tax evasion, and on the distribution of wealth, which is impressive. What we find much less impressive is the Party's claim to put things right if it wins the next election. Apart from being tempted to ask why they didn't do something about these problems during the five years when they were in office, it would be interesting to know how they would propose to both co-operate with, and curb, the directors of the few hundred great combines who to-day, to quote the Labour Party statement, "determine between them what Britain should produce".

> As their power increases, these men, together with the Directors of the leading insurance companies, are usurping the functions of a Government which is theoretically responsible to the whole people . . . The free-enterprise system provides no check to this dangerous trend [of take-overs]. Far from restraining it, the record of the Tories is one of retreat from government by Ministers responsible to Parliament into government by boardroom, responsible to no one.

We have always maintained that the real rulers of the country are not to be found on the Government benches. The Labour Party record in government and its statements in opposition are far from convincing arguments that in office they would be any more successful. But if they succeeded in establishing themselves as the effective government, even more reason for the working people of this country to doubt that any government can serve the people's true interests. For the greater the power of the government the less say have the people in their own affairs.

Full employment, social security in sickness and old age, opportunity, these are words which belong to the vocabulary of the insecure society of capitalism. Leisure, freedom, struggle, living, — belong to a different language which no government, whatever its complexion or the promises it makes, can provide. To move from a society in which production is for profit or is geared to the policies of State, to one in which it is based on needs requires more than a change of government. The Labour Party statement reminds us that "the top 1 per cent. of the population owns nearly half the nation's private wealth and property . . . In 1959 over £6,000 millions were made in untaxed capital gains."

To dislodge such privilege requires something more radical than a change in government personnel.

[July 8, 1961]

ROOM AT THE TOP?

The Labour Party's Election Manifesto, "The New Britain" is an important document; it is not, however, in any sense of the term, a revolutionary manifesto.

An election manifesto by a party strongly "tipped" to win at the polls must obviously aim at winning the votes of the majority of the electorate. Only those parties doomed to defeat can afford extravagant manifestoes and revolutionary programmes. From which we anarchists conclude that the social revolution will never be achieved via the polls. For not only are political programmes revolutionary in inverse ratio to one's chances of vote catching, but equally important, such programmes must be "practical", which means possible within the existing social, political and economic framework.

So when we say that Labour's Manifesto is an important document, we are not also saying that it is so far reaching that anarchists should drop their traditional opposition to voting and give theirs to Mr. Wilson & Co. when the time comes. It is a reformist manifesto *par excellence;* one which the *Guardian* describes as "serious and convincing". What is important and serious is that it raises a number of practical questions which will face a free society no less than existing authoritarian society, as well as offering criticisms of injustices in society as it is, which, apart from confirming many anarchist arguments, reveals that even politicians no longer feel able to treat the public as morons and slaves.

> Labour does not accept that democracy is a five-yearly visit to the polling booth that changes little but the men at the top. We are working for an active democracy, in which men and women as responsible citizens consciously assist in shaping the surroundings in which they live, and take part in deciding how the community's wealth is to be shared among all its members.

Who other than the anarchists could have made enough people self-conscious of the humiliation of the "five-yearly visit" to provoke a denial from Labour that it treats it as such? Equally revealing, and for the same reasons, are the assurances that Labour will seek to "humanise the whole administration of the State" and ensure that "the growth of government activity does not infringe the liberties of the individual" as well as "seeking to establish a true partnership between the people and their parliament". A lot of flannel to get the votes of "thinking" people? Agreed! But we can surely learn something of the political climate and trends from the vote-catching techniques of the parties which, we would suggest, are less blatant, less cock-sure, less demagogical than they were, say, even a generation ago.

To dub all believers in government as authoritarians, power maniacs or sheep, as some anarchists do, is bad for our propaganda, which after all depends for its success on the good faith of those to whom we direct it. We do not find it surprising that most people use their vote (even when they do so with no more illusions than that they are opting for the lesser of two evils), if they can see no alternative to government for the organisation of the day to day existence of the community. Anarchists on the whole, have not, unfortunately, been very effective in presenting the alternative — for a whole number of reasons. In the first place anarchists tend to be reluctant propagandists. Secondly, having understood the political and capitalist rackets, they can, as individuals, more or less live their lives free from both, and they generalise from their own situation into believing that what they can do everybody else could do *if they wished.* They, just as at the other extreme, the capitalist tycoon, can "live their lives" only because they are a small minority. They are both privileged minorities — the millionaire with the power he derives from his control over wealth, the individualist anarchist by the power that comes from knowledge plus philosophy of life — and therefore a world of millionaires or of individualist anarchists would be a physical impossibility.

We are opposed to government because all centralised authority cannot but reduce the individual to a cipher, a statistic. We equally oppose the arrogance of the individualist who declares his self-sufficiency (while enjoying the many services others provide) and who lacks the humility to appreciate that all mankind is not as enlightened as himself.

Whether we like it or not, we anarchists live in a world in which 3,000,000,000 other people have daily material needs just as ourselves; and if we believed that if each one of these three thousand million humans thought as we did everybody would have a square meal every day and the other basic necessities of life, we would deserve to be accused of being "dreamers", "idealists", "utopians".

Whatever socialists and anarchists may have thought in the 19th century about the "idea" of growing the food we consume and uniting us all in brotherhood, anarchist opposition to government is opposition to imposed authority and not to the need for organisation in society. We oppose the Labour Party's "New Britain" election manifesto not because they argue that there must be organisation and planning, but because they fondly imagine that one can achieve "an expanding economy where social justice is seen to prevail" by a number of reforms none of which threatens the principles of the capitalist society, that is, the privileged society. By legislation the Labour Party propose to improve the lot of the poor and give every youngster the chance of rising to the top.

It is true that in the Manifesto one sights an odd moral homily floating in an ocean of financial reforms none of which are even intended to threaten the privileged class. After "thirteen years of Tory rule" and centuries during which a limited few have been sharing out the wealth of the nation among themselves, when the Clores have made their millions and Rachman's heirs have consolidated their property rackets, the promise that a Labour government will be firm about the leftovers after the feast will hardly inspire the bluest-eyed Labour fan. To promise a tightening up of legislation against the monopolists and take-over bidders now, when they have already swallowed each other up, is to close the stable door when the horse has bolted. Obviously the Labour Party cannot be blamed for this state of affairs, but if they meant business they would be seeking their support in the streets and not at the polling booths.

In spite of the fact that the Manifesto actually states the Party's "belief" in the "socialist axiom 'from each according to his ability, to each according to his need'," time and again it is made quite clear that it is by material incentives that "enterprise" will be "stimulated"; just as nowhere does one discover any proposals to deprive the rich of their ill-gotten gains however many plans there are to prevent them from adding to them quite as quickly and as easily as in the past (capital gains tax; public acquisition of land).

Essentially the Manifesto offers tit-bits to the poor, but no way out from their under-privileged economic and social situation. The Labour Party's proposal to abolish the 11-plus gives more people a chance to get to the top, but so long as there is a top there will be a bottom; so at best it will mean that in future the privileged class will emerge from all strata of society instead of from a hereditary ruling class.

[September 19, 1964]

ANOTHER PHONEY WAR?

A week after the Labour Party issued their Manifesto "The New Britain" the Conservatives came out with theirs: "Prosperity with a Purpose". And sandwiched between the two Big Brothers, in time as well as policies, was the Liberals' Manifesto: "Think for Yourself".

Far from making the task of the voter easier, the publication of these Manifestoes presents him with a dilemma, an *embarras de choix* as the French would say, as they feast their eyes on a display of mouth-watering tit-bits, galantines, hors d'oeuvres, chickens in aspic, goose liver and the rest in the delicatessen shop! For, let us face it, each of the three Parties is presenting us with a bill of fare the like of which not even the most optimistic socialist, a mere half century ago, could have promised as the rewards of a socialist Britain without being accused of idealism or just wishful thinking. So, short of the three Parties scrapping their Manifestoes, and issuing a joint one with the promise that the next government will be represented by the leading lights from all three, we suggest that all the voter can do now is to decide which Party he will vote for by using a pin.

After all, the points of disagreement between the Parties are over details which are neither here nor there. Both the Labour and Liberal Parties are in favour of Britain dispensing with her independent nuclear weapons whereas the Tories are in favour of keeping them. This is made into a vital issue by the Conservatives on the grounds that only by having the bomb can we "deter an aggressor". But if this theory were true then the Tory government, instead of seeking to limit membership of the International Nuclear Club to Russia, the United States and Britain, should be advocating that every country be in possession of its independent nuclear deterrent, and, hey presto! peace and goodwill among men would be universal. The fact is that war will only be abolished from the face of the earth when the *causes* as well as the *weapons* of war are removed, and none of the Manifestoes seeks to analyse the *causes* of war, while both the Labour and Liberal Parties propose to increase this country's conventional armament. "The liberals will shift the emphasis to building up our conventional forces, so that Britain can fulfil its world-wide obligations until an effective UN force takes over". "A Labour Government's first concern will be to put our defences on a sound basis and to ensure that the nation gets value for money on its overseas expenditure . . . Our stress will be on the strengthening of our regular conventional forces so that we can contribute our share to NATO defence and also fulfil our peace keeping commitments to the Commonwealth and United Nations." The Tories declare that "over 90 per cent. of our defence effort is devoted to conventional arms . . . but in this nuclear age no money spent on increasing the size or improving the conventional equipment of our forces could by itself secure the defence of these islands."

If the Tories' 90 per cent. is accurate then it can be assumed that the conventional "defence" proposals of both the Liberal and Labour Parties would cost even more than the Tories' 13-year spending spree which, according to the Labour Party, cost £20,000 million and "has left our defence . . . weaker than at any time in our history".

But whatever any of the three Party Manifestoes say about "defence" it is a lot of unadulterated poppycock, for they all not only avoid discussing the *causes* of war but equally remain silent on the role the cold war plays in the economic programmes — for full employment, affluence and all the prosperity they promise the nation. We submit that the cold war is a regulating valve without which the capitalist system could not have functioned without major crises during these twenty post-war years. It is all very well for some economists to say that there would be no financial crisis or mass unemployment if there were world disarmament because the cold war represents only a small percentage of the national product of each country. It is obvious that when we talk of mass unemployment, of economic depressions, we are referring to a situation which still only directly affects a small minority of the working population but which has its repercussions in many sectors of the economy, as well as on the political climate.

The lesson of the inter-war years was not lost on the ruling class after World War II, and it is perhaps worth pointing out that whereas the twenty inter-war years were marked by mass unemployment, Wall Street Crises, record numbers of bankruptcies, and "disarmament", the twenty years since the end of World War II, in spite of at least two Powers possessing the means to obliterate mankind, and massive expenditure on "defence" by most countries which, according to every self-respecting socialist and anarchist in the inter-war years, must inevitably lead to war . . . we are, in this writer's opinion, not in sight of World War III. It is true that there have been all kinds of "minor" wars, but let us not forget that most of them are linked to a far-reaching process of *decolonisation* which also seemed impossible in the inter-war years. Because we believe that the ruling class learned the lessons of the inter-war years, we refuse to take seriously the differences which divide the Labour and

Liberal Parties from the Tory Party on the question of "defence". And since we are also convinced that both the former and the latter base their policies on expert advice it confirms our view that there are very few subjects on which the so-called layman is not as able as the expert to offer an opinion assuming he is given equal access to all the available facts. Take, for instance, the example of Britain's possession of an independent nuclear "deterrent". The Conservative Manifesto declares

> The only effective defence is the certainty in the mind of any enemy that there is no prize he could ever win by our defeat which could compensate him for the destruction he would suffer in the process. Conservatives do not accept the view that we could never be threatened on our own, or that an enemy will always assume we shall have allies rushing to our side. Britain must in the ultimate resort have independently controlled nuclear power to deter an aggressor. We possess the power to deter an aggressor. Only under a Conservative Government will we possess it in the future.

The Liberals, on the other hand, maintain that

> The attempt to maintain an independent British range of nuclear weapons has encouraged the proliferation of nuclear weapons, weakened our economy, and deprived our conventional forces of forces they desperately need.
>
> Liberals will shift the emphasis to building up our conventional forces...

The same view is expressed in the Labour Manifesto which also argues that it is not true

> that all this costly defence expenditure (on Polaris know-how and Polaris missiles from the USA) will produce an 'independent British deterrent'. It will not be independent and it will not be British and it will not deter. Its possession will impress neither friend nor potential foe...
>
> The Government bases its policy on the assumption that Britain must be prepared to go it alone without her allies in an all-out thermo-nuclear war with the Soviet Union, involving the obliteration of our people. By constantly reiterating this appalling assumption the Government is undermining the alliance on which our security now depends.

Such diametrically opposed policies can only indicate that either the whole business of defence is just a wild speculation, and that one theory is as good as any other, or they have nothing to do with defence but a lot to do with economic theories and interests, and with influential pressure groups. If the policiticans were really concerned with defence the first step they would take is to arm the people, whereas this is always the last thing governments will consider doing. The second step would be to limit arms production to a nation's needs, whereas in fact countries such as Britain actually export war material.

Perhaps it is no longer true to say that "Death (the war industry) Pays Dividends", in the sense that it did in the old days to a handful of industrialists and financial tycoons. To-day the cold war provides employment for millions of workers and professional men for whom peace and disarmament would mean unemployment and the loss of well remunerated jobs. In other words, there are millions of petty vested interests in the war industry to buttress the capitalist system's need for a cold-war economy. For those who have a vested interest as well as for those who really feel strongly on the issue of nuclear weapons versus conventional ones, their votes can matter. But for those of us who are concerned with living and not with choosing between possible death by radiation or roasting, by suffocation or by being blown to smithereens, there is nothing to choose between the Parties. Refusal to vote for these "merchants of death" is a first, necessary small step in the direction of peace.

[September 26, 1964]

SOME REFLECTIONS ON NATIONALISATION

Nationalisation, whatever the intentions of the Labour pioneers may have been, means neither workers' control nor public ownership, since those working in nationalised industries, as well as the consumers, have no say in their management.

In theory a nationalised industry should be one in which the best possible service for the public and conditions for those working in that industry are combined. In fact there is a centralisation, a de-personalisation at the top against which neither worker nor consumer has any redress. A footplateman with 36 years experience put it succinctly in an interview with the *News Chronicle* last week: "Frankly, many things are worse than before nationalisation: too much red tape and waste of money. Our contact with the Commission is remote. The only information we get about it is through its monthly magazine."

And users of public transport were baldly informed in the middle of the present strike that fares are going up to the tune of some £25 million in the next 12 months.

An election issue was the Labour Party's proposed nationalisation of the Chemical Industry, including the I.C.I. empire (with sales figures in 1954 of £352 millions and net profits amounting to £21.7 millions). In a telegram to a Conservative candidate the Minister of Fuel and Power confirmed that

> . . . as a consequence of the nationalisation of the gas industry, profit-sharing schemes for 50,000 employees came to an end. Some of these schemes dated back to 1889, and thus nearly seventy years of industrial progress were swept aside.
>
> The basis of nationalisation is non-profit-making state ownership. Since there are no profits, there cannot be profit-sharing. Thus, the nationalisation of the chemical industry must inevitably have the same effect as that in the gas industry.

One of the troubles with Nationalised industries is that they are run as profit-making concerns (the Labour leaders insist that they "must pay their way"); that in fact the five Nationalised industries made a profit in 1953 of £137 millions of which £109 millions went into the pockets of former shareholders in the shape of interest and compensation.

Nationalised industries have not changed the status of workers engaged in them. The Boss has been replaced by the State. In the circumstances, therefore, the worker is in a weaker position for bargaining since the principal weapon at his disposal — the strike — has lost much of its force. An individual employer can hold out against the demands of striking workers for a limited time, the State indefinitely, as well as possessing powers to introduce Emergency Measures (legalised blacklegging) in the name of the Community. Nationalisation without workers' control, therefore, is a retrograde step as far as workers are concerned.

Private enterprise — or what is left of it by the Combines — by its competitive basis cannot ignore the consumer entirely (how foolish the public has been in not forming Consumers' Unions!). Nationalisation without the direct participation of the Consumer is uniformity and totalitarianism.

Can Nationalisation — taken to mean *public ownership* in the fullest sense of the word — co-exist with free enterprise and the Conservative "property-owning democracy"? We think not. Either free enterprise is allowed to survive in which case Nationalisation will, as is the case to-day, be a large scale model of free enterprise with all its defects and none of its advantages. Or if Nationalisation is really public ownership then "free enterprise" faces complete bankruptcy. For apart from considerations of efficiency, service and working conditions, it would mean the end of the profit motive in production, the *raison d'etre* of "free enterprise".

The pursuit of a thoroughgoing policy of Nationalisation must result either in an equalitarian society in which money, as we know it to-day, will have become redundant, or in the all powerful, totalitarian State with a new class structure, new inequalities and new injustices.*

In either eventuality most of the privileged members of our society risk losing their power and private fortunes. Private enterprise's reply is to save what it can and consolidate what is left. Hence the growing number of mergers of companies** (their own kind of nationalisation with which they proceed apace whilst paying lip-service to private enterprise) and the development of profit-sharing schemes for employees (I.C.I. for instance last year credited 75,000 employees with a bonus equal to a shilling in the pound of their wages — that is a total of £2,500,000 — which will be used to buy shares in the Company for the wage earners). The purpose of such schemes does not need elaborating, and if the workers fall for it the bosses kill *three* birds with one stone.

Capitalism, Trade Unionism, Socialism . . all are at the cross-roads. Their spokesmen will seek to salvage what they can from the shambles they have created; a bit of nationalisation and a differential here and less taxation on profits and more productivity there. But none will admit that the only way of dealing with a shambles is to clear it away and start afresh with new ideas and values based on the commonweal.

[June 11, 1955]

*"To hear tell around Kazakhstan, some Soviet farmers are getting rich under the new order of agriculture instituted by the Communist party in 1953.

According to the regional government headquarters in Akmolinsk, fifteen members of collective farms in the region have made applications for Zim limousines. That is equivalent to saying that fifteen Kansas wheat farmers have placed orders for private yachts.

The Zim, a seven-passenger limousine, not conspicuously suitable for the dirt roads of the Akmolinsk countryside, is the second largest Soviet automobile. It costs 42,000 rubles, or nearly five times the annual average wage of a Soviet worker as calculated by foreign economists. (At the official rate of exchange, there are four rubles to the dollar.)

A few farmers in the Akmolinsk region, government authorities say, collected 70,000 to 75,000 rubles each last year, or eight to nine times the average wage." *(New York Times,* May 3.)

** Business mergers in America are up 200% over 1949 according to the Federal Trade Commission.

2
"Bevanism" or the Power Struggle

WATCH MR. FOOT, MR. BEVAN & CO.

If the struggles within the Labour Party represented an open revolt against the parliamentary system in general, and the quasi-dictatorial powers of the Labour Party-Trade Union executives in particular, we could find ourselves working up some enthusiasm over the events on the home front during the past fortnight. But in fact the Attle-Bevan battle is being fought within the prison walls of parliamentary democracy.

"Are we making Parliament a Sham?" asks Michael Foot in last week's issue of *Tribune*, and, using similar arguments to the ones we have advanced recently, demonstrates in a most convincing way that this is the case. He does not pause, however, to question parliamentary democracy, but seeks a scapegoat in the Labour Party Standing Orders. Mr. Foot in spite of his experience does not question the principle of government; he even wishes us to believe that "the people can participate in the government" if only they are "put in a position to judge the conduct of their representatives". All that is necessary is that "the proceedings of parliament should be conducted in the open, that both the debates there and the voting lists shuld be made public".

Mr. Foot quotes extensively and with approval from the writings of Edmund Burke, and his choice reveals that the only revolutions Mr. Foot will join are palace revolutions; not for him the street!

Mr. Foot believes in 'public men' — however much Mr. Bevan may deplore, in another column of *Truune*, that mankind should "hold its breath on the edge of the precipice until the British Prime Minister [Churchill] recovered from his partial paralysis" — and what is more, for him "parliament without parties to-day would become a rabble incapable of accomplishing anything". (Can one imagine how horrified Mr. Foot would be at the suggestion that the destinies of the country should be in the hands of the people, all fifty million of them?) He quotes Burke in defence of party politics: "When bad men combine the good must associate; else they will fall one by one, an unpitied sacrifice in a contemptible struggle". A very good quotation which anarchists could quote as well as Mr. Foot, the only difference being that he assumes — against all the evidence — that there are good politicians, whereas the anarchist contends that the people can only defend themselves where they are strongest, not through "representatives" in Parliament but at their places of work, in their affinity groups, and in larger groupings where organisation is spontaneous and controlled from below.

Mr. Foot quotes Burke in defence of "action" at all costs:

> "All virtue which is impracticable, said Burke, is spurious. We should rather run the risk of falling into faults in a course which leads us to act with effect and energy than to loiter out our days without blame and without use. Public life is a situation of power and energy; 'he trespasses against his duty who sleeps upon his watch, as well as he who goes over to the enemy'." This, as I have said, is the classical defence of the party system . . . Certainly I dissent from not one word of it.

Not the wilderness for Mr. Foot and his friends! They seek the limelight and power, and time is pressing for these middle-aged politicians thwarted by old men, and threatened by a bunch of ambitious, up-and-coming yes-men. Their only hope lies in the exploitation of the goodwill and aspirations of the rank and file of the Labour Party and the Trade Union movement since the Party and Union machines are in the Attlee bag.

But let no working man or liberally-minded person be misled into confusing means with ends. For the Bevanites the goal is political power, and if, and when, they occupy the government benches they will conduct affairs in much the same way as their predecessors. Their means — their tactic — is cunning and dangerous, for they appeal to, and pose as, the real champions of the common man. Yet when the people should dare to voice their criticisms they will treat them as "a rabble" just as Mr. Foot has suggested Parliament would become once Members voted according to the dictates of their conscience (or according to the wishes of their constituents?).

No action is possible without running the risk of making mistakes. Agreed. But in the first place action which is in contradiction with one's fundamental principles is doomed in advance to failure and disaster. Secondly, it is one thing to be responsible for the consequences of one's actions, quite another to have to shoulder the consequences of the actions of others in which one has had no voice. This is the tragedy of the political systems of to-day.

The issue of *Tribune* before us is essential reading for those who may harbour illusions or pin their hopes on the Bevanite group or in parliamentary democracy. They have nothing to offer which any other group of politicians could not offer equally well. Their hopes of peace rest on the meeting table around which the Big Three will thrash out their differences. Bevan's article is an attack on the vanity of Churchill on the one hand and a call for a meeting of Churchill and the leaders of the great powers on the other. He does not look to the workers of the world to end the tension. On the contrary he is fostering the view that "the ordinary men and women throughout the world are *looking to their statesmen for courage and sagacity* — and endless patience" (our italics) . . . And oh! if only they had the good sense to put Nye Bevan in power. And Michael Foot in a straight-from-the-shoulder attack on parliamentary democracy, which he confesses is both a "sham" and a "farce", has nevertheless neither offered any suggestions as to how the voice of the people might, under a Foot-Bevan regime, play a dominating role in their deliberations, nor has he decided to resign from that talking shop of which he surely despairs when he asks:

> What is the use of judgement which can effect no votes, thought which can influence no one else's thinking, a speech which may satisfy a man's conscience or ego but which cannot affect the action of his audience?

Poor, twisted, Mr. Foot! Is he really so naive or does he think his readers that stupid?

[March 19, 1955]

THE BEVAN BLAST

Whether Mr. Bevan, as some journalists say, is politically "finished" or not, his utterances are still front page news both for the *News of the World* and the *Manchester Guardian.* His speech at Manchester last Saturday shows that he has little to learn from his colleagues in the techniques of the politician, and that within the blinkered horizons of parliamentary "socialism" *they* probably have a lot to learn from him. But what does all Mr. Bevan's agitation boil down to if not that the leadership of the Labour Party is in the *wrong* hands? To one questioner he pointed out that to leave the Labour Party because it was in the hands of the most "reactionary members" was a "gospel of despair". "You never know what is going to happen in politics" — he continued, with a smile. "You are up to-day and out to-morrow, or out to-day and in to-morrow," and he instanced his own career: of being expelled from the party in 1939 and six years later finding himself a Cabinet Minister in the Labour Government. This is all very illuminating for those who, like Mr. Bevan, are "interested in being a leader", but what this has to do with socialism is difficult to fathom.

His comments on personal success affecting individual judgement were interesting. He said:

> If the Labour Party is not going to be a socialist party, I don't want to lead it. I don't believe you can measure the progress of society by the individual careers. I know of so many people who imagine a society has succeeded because they have succeeded in it.

But surely this is the strongest argument against party politics, for with few exceptions — which do not include Mr. Bevan — the aim of politicians is to win power for their party and a job (with prospects) for themselves in the government. The Labour Party's six years in office (plus the war years in the coalition) has produced all the evils of which Mr. Bevan complains, and there is therefore something cynical in his reported statement that "It was only those who suffered under society who wanted to change it, and these people, in the main, were Labour's 'gathering grounds' ", for obviously the leaders of the Party and of the Trade Unions can by no stretch of the imagination be described as the victims of society. What they are doing, in fact, is to use these people to further their careers as politicians. That there are ordinary workers to-day who vote conservative tells us less of the mentality of the voters than it does of the socialist appeal of the Labour Party.

Mr. Bevan also said some hard things about the decadence of liberal journalism in this country:

It was the first time in the history of Liberal thought that it had ranged itself on the side of what had come to be known as the establishment — the accepted order of things: the vested interests: the big, all-powerful battalions. We expected liberalism to be astringent, questioning and, if necessary, rebellious. One of the reasons why political thinking in Great Britain was so bad — and bad it was — was because that astringency had gone out.

But why single out Liberal journalism for these attacks. What of Mr. Bevan's own journal, *Tribune* (whose editor, Mr. Edwards, very quietly, and without a word in *Tribune,* left to join Lord Beaverbrook's *Evening Standard*)? The only "astringency" one finds in the Bevanite organ is in its clipped journalism in the much-despised *Daily Mirror* style. It also shares with the *Daily Mirror* the boosting and damming of personalities and the sensational approach. But where is the "questioning", the "political thinking", the self-criticism that one might expect following Mr. Bevan's Manchester outburst? Indeed the front page article in last week's issue is by the great man himself and is full of smug self-satisfaction about the findings of the Committee of Inquiry which has reported favourably on the Health Service, inaugurated when Bevan was Minister of Health. Without denying him his share in "This Famous Victory" (*Tribune's* title), is it not beating the drum a little too loudly to present him, as *Tribune* does this week in bold letters, as "Aneurin Bevan, the man who fought the opposition of the Rothermeres, the Kemsleys, the Dains, the Hills and all the others". Certainly it does not seem to be the best way to encourage the rank and file to act and think for themselves with such a David just waiting to be called to fight their battles for them!

But what, apart from the direct issue of personal power, divides Bevan from the present leadership of the Labour Party? His attacks on the secrecy of the parliamentary party meetings, at which decisions are taken without consultation with the rank-and-file, are not over questions of principle but of tactics: "If it [the secrecy] goes or *it is the end of parliamentary institutions",* and Mr. Bevan ("I am not a Communist. I am a democratic Socialist") believes in "transforming society from institutions based upon private property and private exploitation into industries based on public service", presumably through the "parliamentary institutions" which he is so anxious to preserve. In other words a concentration of all power in the hands of the State.

Gaitskell's approach, it would appear, is to achieve some kind of "equality" by a wider distribution of capital and the creation of machinery to prevent the further accumulation of capital in a few hands as at present. This would be achieved by the State acquiring an increasing interest in industry and as a result, in managing the reinvestment of capital without, however, necessarily controlling the actual management of industry. From the point of view of an old-fashioned social-democrat such as Bevan ("I didn't join the Labour Party. I grew up in it") who sees nationalisation as the solution to all our troubles, Gaitskell's "re-thinking" is a move to the Right. But in fact neither is very much to the Left and both of them would run their "socialist" society with government and State capitalism.

Of course these "socialists" overlook what are the essentials, from the point of view of social justice, and for very good reasons, since they are politicians ("I am not interested in being the leader of any party, but merely in being a leader" — Bevan at Manchester). Classes exist because a minority section of society has power over the lives of the majority. The evil of money is a real evil in capitalist society because it is the means by which to-day a relatively small number of individuals can determine the way millions of others shall live their lives. In other words the injustice as we see it is not that a few thousand families can afford to relieve the boredom of their lives with luxuries but the *power* which their wealth at present gives them to control or jeopardise *our* lives. For anarchists the distinction is fundamental; not so for the Labour Party "socialists".

Assuming they mean what they say when they talk about economic equality, they seek to achieve it nevertheless by concentrating more and more power in the hands of the State. Thus theoretically it would be possible to abolish the money system altogether, and yet there would still be classes and with all our 'equality' we should be slaves! In practice, as "Soviet" Russia teaches, even where the economy is controlled by the State the money system continues to be used as a means for creating classes within the ruled class, of dividing loyalties, of holding out the carrot of hope of advancement for the slaves with "ambition". For no ruling class can survive in a community united by a common and equal injustice (which explains why 500 united Smithfield market 'bummarees' are more effective than 500,000 railway workers divided by wage differentials and craft unionism).

Whatever Bevan may say of the moral bases of socialism *the instrument* for its achievement is from above: the State, the politician, the government:

Socialism was not merely an economic theory, but a way of life. Economists came into it when you were seeking means of carrying out your central purpose which must first of all be based on a moral decision, not merely on one arrived at by considering this and that and finding what was possible. Any statesman who concerned himself with what was possible never did anything. Statesmanship was an act of continuous creation, and creation meant bringing something new into life.

And this goes too for the theoreticians of the movement. Even such "rebels" as Professor G.D.H. Cole, in spite of being the leader of the newly created World Socialist Movement, offers nothing new. In the last of his series of articles on *What is Wrong with the Trade Unions?* (Tribune, Feb 3, 1956) he puts forward a hotch-potch of revolutionary ("to talk of Socialism without confiscation has always been nonsense"), Gaitskellian and Bevanite ideas which can only create despair as well as confusion in the minds of his readers.

Thus:

All Socialists wish to expropriate the capitalists somehow: even those who wish to pay compensation have every intention of cancelling it in the long run. Most Trade Union leaders, however, have not yet fully appreciated the logic of the situation: they see only that they cannot go all out for higher wages under capitalism, and have not seen that the remedy is to do away with capitalism now instead of allowing their aspirations to be stultified by its continuance.

Nor have most of their members seen this; for many of them still believe that wages and consumption could be increased at the expense of profits, whereas in practice high wages and high profits go together, as the Labour Government discovered while it was in office after 1945.

The delusion is possible because few workers are investors in industry or realise the indispensability of high investment to the future prosperity and level of employment in this country. Here again, the only remedy is more and better Trade Union education to bring home the hard economic facts and prevent Trade Unionists from being deluded by over-optimistic false prophets.

This education is needed, not in order to persuade Trade Unionists to acquiesce in 'wage restraint' in the interest of profit-making, but to bring home to them how indispensable it is to transfer these profits from the present owners to the public, and to get and sustain in power Governments that will ensure that the benefit of rising productivity accrues to the workers as fast as more can be spared from the requirements of *public* investment.

The "re-thinking" which the last Labour Party conference undertook as its task between now and the next elections is for Bevan a sinister Gaitskellian conspiracy.

You would have thought that some of those men had only just arrived in the Socialist movement. You would have thought that the history of the Socialist Movement began when they came into it. The history of the Socialist movement looks as though it is beginning to end when they came into it.

One can understand Mr. Bevan's feelings in the matter. But he is behaving as a sentimentalist while Mr. Gaitskell is the realist. Social democracy in Europe which began its career in the Centre has, through the years, steadily shifted to the Right (Mr. Bevan with it), as was inevitable. And the Right has by the force of circumstance as well as in its own interests (with the guidance of the industrial psychologists and the pressures from the Unions) moved towards the Centre. Capitalism is still a powerful ruling force in society; social democracy is as dead as mutton. The only re-thinking the workers can profitably engage in must be based on a post-mortem on the corpse of social democracy and not on the assumption that it can be revived from the dead. Social democracy is dead because "government by-for-and of-the people" has been proved once for all a myth; because power corrupts all who wield it; because the means are never justified by the ends (even assuming these to be noble and just); *because the social revolution will never be achieved through the ballot box.*

The re-thinking of the working classes must be as revolutionary in its particular sphere as is the present re-thinking in science and industry. The Gaitskell economists are seeking the formula which will inject capitalism with new masters as well as give it a new lease of life. The alternative is nothing less than *economic and social freedom through freedom!*

[February 11, 1956]

Mr. FOOT'S 'BEAUTIFUL MORNING'!

Splashed across the front page of last week's *Tribune* is a three-line headline which reads: "Oh! What a Beautiful Morning" and of course it had nothing to do with the weather but referred to the election of Mr. Bevan to the treasurership of the Labour Party, an event which the writer of the article, Michael Foot, considers the "happiest political occasion" he could remember "since that great day in 1945 when the Labour Government was returned to power with a thumping majority".

Both Mr. Foot and Mr. Bevan (the latter at the *Tribune* meeting in Blackpool) put forward the line that Bevan's election was "a victory for Labour's rank-and-file". What a lot of oratorical nonsense this all is, is made clear by reading Mr. Foot's article.

He tells us that the "gospel of defeatism" was a "deadly doctrine" which Labour's rank-and-file refused to accept.

> Time and again they revolted. But time and again they were crushed — thanks to the power which the operation of Labour's Constitution seemed to bestow into the hands of a few. A clique appeared to usurp the functions of leadership; they had it all their own way.

It was, he says, to combat "the peril of cynicism and despair" spreading far and wide throughout the country that "Aneurin Bevan decided to abandon the certainty of election in the constituency party section for all the risks involved in a fight for the Treasurer-ship". Three times did crusader Bevan attack the infidels' citadel, and on his last attempt (thanks to the backing of some of the infidels) his efforts have been crowned with success.

Now Michael Foot recognises that if Labour "is to call itself a democratic Party" a reform in the Constitution itself was one requirement. Yet he tells us that the reform, whereby the women's section on the Executive would be abolished and the Trade Unions and constituency parties equally represented, was rejected, thereby indicating that the votes which returned Bevan to the treasurership were not available when it was a question of reforming the Constit-ution — or rather, of lessening the stranglehold of the Unions on the Party's policies. If the election of Bevan was the expression of the "rank-and-file" how was it that it was able to express itself on one matter and not on an equally important one in what Mr. Bevan called the "shift to the Left of the central direction of the party"?

Before attempting to answer this question let us examine other aspects of Mr. Foot's "beautiful morning". At last year's elections for the treasurership Mr. Bevan was faced by a prominent figure in the Party — indeed the man who later stepped into Mr. Attlee's shoes as leader of the Party — and in a straight fight Bevan polled only 1,225,000 votes compared with 5,475,000 for Mr. Gaitskell. In this year's election there were four candidates, of whom Mr. Bevan — in spite of his protests that "far too much attention has been given to personalities" — was undoubtedly the most outstanding.

As it was he polled less than half the "votes" (3,029,500 against a combined total of 3,441,000 for his opponents) and the new votes did not come from the constituency parties, which had already voted for him last year, but from a few of the large Unions which had previously voted against him. Thus the block vote which had been his downfall last year, and which, says Mr. Foot, is the stumbling-block to "real democracy in the Party", was responsible for Mr. Bevan's victory — "symbolic of a shift of opinion inside the Labour Party" — and for Mr. Foot's "beautiful morning"!

At the Press conference called by Mr. Bevan after his election he was asked a most pertinent question: "What do you think of the block vote now?" He replied with that *sang-froid,* cynicism and hypocrisy common to all politicians: "I consider that, in some respects, the block vote has adjusted itself to the point of view of the rank and file".

That Bevan's Blackpool "success" (coupled with the emergence of Mr. Cousins) has generally been interpreted as "a shift to the Left", in fact means very little. Left or Right have lost their meaning, so much so that in the last elections the electorate was hard pressed to distinguish between the policies of the Conservatives and of Labour. The apparent optimism at Blackpool was more likely due to a feeling that the Conservative government was "on the run" over its disastrous foreign policy and its inability to square the circle of capitalist economics, than to a breath of fresh air (from the Left) blowing away the cautious, unadventurous policies of the old men of the Labour movement.

The purpose of conferences so far as opposition parties are concerned is to win elections (even the Liberals' leader told the assembly that they had not met simply *to talk* but *to win votes* at the next election). And though there may be heated discussions as to the best policies to secure the maximum number of votes, "unity" is perhaps the most powerful electioneering weapon in the political parties' armouries. It may well be that such considerations account for the pro-Bevan block votes at Blackpool.

But when Michael Foot writes that Blackpool has brought that "dream" (to secure a new Labour Government pledged to a forthright socialistic policy) much nearer to reality he is either indulging in pure demagogy or else is just plain silly.

In the first place it would be necessary to redefine Socialism — for, even as understood by *Tribune's* stormy petrels, it would make the Pioneers turn in their graves. But leaving aside what our practical socialists — "but we could not wait for ideal solutions" — might call academic considerations, the fact remains that in the Labour Party it is the tail which wags the dog. But that is not all. The Labour movement — the Party and the Trade Unions — which exists to advance the cause of the worker, the underdog, is so constituted that the underdog has virtually no say in its policy decisions. Bevan declares that he regards election to the treasurership as "symbolical, that is to say to try and determine how far the movement has the capacity to adjust itself to varying moods of the movement".

But it is also symbolical of the hierarchical structure of the movement and is perpetuated when a Bevan stands for election. In his speech at the *Tribune* meeting Bevan is reported as having said that: "It is extremely dangerous when political institutions are too far separated from the people. This week we have, to some extent, rectified that mistake". *How far,* we wonder, should they be separated for Mr. Bevan's liking?

Just as the struggle between Labour and Conservative politicians is essentially one of power, so within the Labour movement, the disunity between the Party and the Unions is fundamentally a power struggle between the Trade Union leaders and the Labour Party politicians. "Unity" at Blackpool simply means that for the common purpose of winning elections the two leaderships are prepared to seek a *modus vivendi.* But the Welfare and happiness of the working people for which these organizations ostensibly exist are of secondary importance, or at most stepping stones for political careerists. And it matters little whether their name is Gaitskell or Bevan . . . or even Michael Foot.

[October 13, 1956]

THE 'SAGACITY' OF THE HON. MR. BEVAN, P.C.

At the height of the Attlee-Bevan struggle more than two years ago we wrote a piece with the title "Watch Mr. Foot, Mr. Bevan & Co." in which we refused to see in these factional struggles any glimmer of hope in a progressive sense.

Last week at the Labour Party's conference Aneurin Bevan, recently returned from his tour of the Capitals of the Near- and Far-East, from a successful dress rehearsal as Shadow Foreign Minister for the next Labour Government, speaking on International Relations and in particular about Labour's attitude to the H-bomb, may have created alarm and despondency among his followers, but from our point of view, as our editorial of two years ago was predicting, he was simply running true to form. He has shown the "courage and sagacity" which, as he wrote at the time, he considers the essential virtues of the "statesman".

By "courage", his followers are only now discovering, he meant the politician's brazen-faced betrayal of his friends in his giddy ascent of the coveted rungs of power.

> "I have thought anxiously about the subject. I knew I was going to make a speech which would offend and even hurt many of my friends." This was greeted by a great roar of "Hear, hear," and Mr. Bevan was stung to shout back: "Do you think I am afraid? I should say what I believe. I don't care what happens".

By "sagacity" they are now realising is meant not principled wisdom but the awareness that when you are in power you cannot behave as an "irresponsible" popular agitator; soap-box oratory and front-bench slickness don't mix. "Sagacity" in politics is the ability to carry on where your predecessor left off; it's the recognition that politics is a vested interest, and the diplomatic world a closed shop.

"If the Executive Committee had asked me to get up and support the hydrogen bomb" — Bevan told the the delegates — "I would have refused". Indeed, had he not "probably made more speeches to more people condemning the bomb" than anyone present? He was as "strongly against it as ever". So nobody should misunderstand him. Firstly, the Party was committed, if returned to power, to "take the initiative in suspending tests". But it was one thing to give a lead to the other Powers by a unilateral suspension of tests, and quite another if this country were to scrap its stocks of nuclear weapons or have nothing to do with those countries, allies as well as potential "enemies", which were working on these weapons of destruction. In that case, said Mr. Bevan, the Statesman,

> You will have to say at once that all international commitments offered to friends and allies must be immediately destroyed . . .
> What this conference ought not to do is to decide on demolishing the whole fabric of British international relations without putting anything in its place.
> To pass the motion would mean that "you will send the British Foreign Secretary naked into the conference chamber".

Later he declared that if the Norwood motion were accepted "It would place a British Foreign Secretary in diplomatic purdah". Mr. Bevan's pre-occupation with the Foreign Secretary's political attire — or lack of it — read in conjunction with the following extract from the report of his speech:

> Mr. Bevan here interrupted his main theme to say that some of the newspapers had interpreted some of his recent actions as being dominated by nothing but a desire to be Foreign Secretary himself, and when someone from the hall cried "Hear, hear" to this he said: "That is a pretty bitter thing to say about me. I would never do anything I did not believe in".

reveals a personal concern with his own power, and his place in history, in the event of a Labour victory at the next elections. It is quite clear, in spite of his denials, that Mr. Bevan is at present Labour's Foreign Secretary designate as well as wanting the job as the next best thing to being Prime Minister designate, or even as a stepping stone to that more exalted post to which he may yet attain if the "statesmanlike" qualities he revealed at Brighton (which converted such an implacable enemy as the *Manchester Guardian* into a qualified admirer) are further developed between now and the general elections. "Unity" in political parties is no more than a marriage of convenience between ambitious, ruthless, vain men and women. One cannot better describe the atmosphere than did James Cameron in his report on the Conference in last Friday's *News Chronicle* when he wrote of the Executive "from the councils of State on the tribune came the quiet rasping sound of axes being ground, the gentle sigh of knives being delicately inserted into backs".

The arguments used by Mr. Bevan for rejecting the Norwood motion for unilateral abolition of the H-bomb were no more original than those advanced by the Tories or by Mr. Churchill when he announced to the House more than two years ago that Britain was working on the H-bomb. Compare Mr. Churchill's

> Personally I cannot feel that we should have much influence over their (the United States) policy or action, wise or unwise, while we are largely dependent upon their protection. We too must possess substantial deterrent power of our own

with Bevan's argument at Brighton last week that:

> Unfortunately the United States and the Soviet Union were in possession of the weapon and we were in danger of extermination as a consequence. *I would like to have the opportunity of exerting an influence on the policies of those countries.* But this (the Norwood motion) is not the way to do it. (Our italics)

Thus both Churchill and Bevan believe that Britain can only influence the Big Two and prevent them from starting an H-war, as a result of which "this country would be poisoned with the rest of mankind" by a show of arms — of H-bombs made-in-Britain. We just cannot see how mankind will be saved as a result of Britain's possession of the Bomb. *Either* an H-bomb war, which every scientist in the world believes *will definitely* or *might* (depending on their political independence or commitment) destroy all mankind, has already been ruled out by the leaders of East and West, in which case Foreign Secretary designate Bevan would be as influential or ineffectual in the international game of politics whether he is naked or clothed in an H-bomb; *or* such a suicidal war has not been ruled out as a possibility in the Power struggle, in which case the possession by Britain of the ultimate weapon can only add to the dangers of extermination.

The H-bomb is either ineffectual, in which case the sooner it is scrapped the better, or it is a threat. It can never be a deterrent without being a threat to mankind, since its effectiveness as a deterrent implies that in the last resort it will be used, and the moment it is used mankind is threatened with annihilation. We cannot escape from the bitter logic of this argument. When Bevan and the Labour Executive attempt to do so it is for other reasons than the future of mankind.

The Labour Party Conference at Brighton was, in fact, committed to evolving a programme that would *win votes* at the next election and not one of seeking to put forward a policy for the commonweal. With this end in mind the Executive soft-pedalled on Nationalisation and refused to take an unequivocal stand against the H-bomb as an instrument of policy. Listen to one of Mr. Bevan's arguments for rejecting the Norwood motion:

> Mr. Bevan said he was profoundly convinced that nothing would give more anxiety to many people who did not share their political views than if the British nation disengaged itself from its obligations and its influence in international affairs.

There are many people in this country who would feel great anxiety if Mr. Bevan were to become Prime Minister. Does Mr. Bevan consider this a valid argument for retiring from the political arena? We hardly think so. Then why does he show concern for those who "do not share our political views", etc. . . if not because he and his colleagues are themselves "anxious" to get their votes at the next elections?

Whatever Lord Pakenham may say about the Conference (in last Sunday's *Observer)* as the most significant since 1935, we are convinced that James Cameron is nearer the mark when he described it as "a flood of anaesthetic oratory, the relentless march of the worn-out phrase and the cliche rubbed smooth by years of indefatigable use". Of course there is going to be a lot of heart-searching and explaining away in *Tribune* offices during the next few weeks. In one speech the great man has knocked the "Bevan" out of Bevanite. Still Mr. Foot and his friends have only themselves to blame for that. They can't say they had not been warned of the dangers of the Cult of the Personality and yet they persisted in building up farmer Nye as the man sent by Providence. And now he has let them down. But who knows, Mr. Foot is probably chuckling away to himself in his office as he doodles with the word "Foot":

Brutus and Caesar; what should be in that "Caesar"?
  Why should that name be sounded more than yours?
Write them together, yours is as fair a name;
  Sound them, it doth become the mouth as well;
Weigh them, it is as heavy; conjure with 'em,
  "Foot" will start a spirit as soon as "Bevan".
Now, in the name of all the gods at once,
  Upon what meat doth this our Bevan feed,
That he is grown so great! . . .

"H'm," — says Michael as he approaches the office mirror, jaw thrust forward, chest expanded to capacity — "and why not?"

[October 12, 1957]

BEVAN'S 'OPPOSITION'

The Labour Party pundits did their best to make political capital out of the futile NATO conference held in Paris. Before Parliament adjourned for the Christmas holidays a debate on Foreign Affairs, which gave Bevan a chance to condemn the H-bomb (after making sure at Brighton that the future Foreign Secretary would have it to 'negotiate' with), ended with a majority vote for the Government of only 38. The Liberals voted with Labour. And six of the seven Tory Independents abstained.

Riding the wave of public fear the Labour and Liberal M.P.s demanded an end to American air patrols over Britain with nuclear bombs on board, and for British control of rocket bases in this country. The punch was taken out of the protest by the reminder that it was the Labour Party when in office which was responsible for the making of American bases in Britain, a point which was conceded by Bevan who claimed that *the situation had now changed.*

The Prime Minister stated that not only were bombs flown in by American aircraft before 1951, but they were also flown in in exercises in machines based in this country. Further disclosures seemed to indicate that the Government was not entirely informed about what the American Air Force was actually doing.

Many people who are afraid of the consequences of Britain being made a nuclear base controlled by the Americans will unfortunately read into the Labour Party protest a hopeful message of peace, thus concluding that the Labour Party is unlikely (or less likely) to engage in military adventures. Nothing could be further from the truth. Neither party is anxious to go to war while the threat of superior retaliation is held by the Soviet Union. But apart from this the history of the Labour Party is not one of militant pacifism. Their object is to get into power and they will exploit any popular feeling, which at the moment happens to be fear of nuclear war, in an attempt to win support. When they formed a coalition under Churchill in 1940 they were not concerned with the international socialists who had been educated in the principle that all wars between competing states are fought for economic reasons.

When Bevan claims that the situation has now changed from the time when Labour was in power and allowed American bases to be set up in this country, his meaning is clear enough to us. The change is that Labour is no longer in power! Intelligent political students know that before any political party puts on "the mantle of responsibility" it is at its most militant and radical.

In addition to his duties to the party Bevan has another reason for his present opposition to the Government's specific defence policy. Many sad Bevan supporters deplored his reversal of policy at the Labour Party Annual Conference: what better method then of winning back their allegiance and affection is there than by exploiting the stupid blunderings of the Tories? But if we examine the statements made in Parliament in his opposition speech they don't amount to very much. What super-patriot would disagree with the sentiment that 'we' should have sovereign claim over nuclear bases? And any good Tory will agree when he says: "We are prepared to abrogate British sovereignty for an overriding international purpose, but not merely to add to the sovereign power of another nation".

The 'international purpose' can be interpreted in many ways.

We take no especial pride in seeing through the carefully selected words of politicians' speeches, because we have experienced the difficulties of persuading people (even those who see the contradictions) that awareness is not enough.

There is general acceptance of the theory that an orderly society must be organised through a privileged power group backed up by force. The faults in our society are sometimes as much the responsibility of the majority of ordinary people as of those who are in power over them.

As long as the myth persists that there are special kinds of men, who, if given power, will dispense justice, peace and equality, then we must continue on our crazy course.

We see signs that more and more people are developing cynical attitudes to Government, but we do not see much evidence that logical conclusions are being drawn from the behaviour of governments.

If the Labour Party is returned to office in the next general election it will not mean that we are embarking on a new era of enlightenment; in our view it will merely indicate that some people think a change of government may bring them nearer to what they want. Their wants may range from cheaper food to the abolition of prison sentences for homosexuals, and while we think that these are reasonable wants we also know that their attainment will be subject to economic and political conditions.

What however is lacking most of all behind the decisions taken on which way to vote, is vision.

[January 4, 1958]

SOCIALISM IN A WHEELCHAIR

The unbridled vanity of politicians as well as their utter contempt for their followers was well demonstrated last Sunday at the Labour Party and T.U.C. rally in Trafalgar Square when at the close of the meeting Bevan, whose principal theme had been that of "Unity", rushed to the microphone dragging Gaitskell with him and cried out "Let us put the coping stone on this great meeting". He called for three cheers "and we'll lead it," he added. Gaitskell, his arm held aloft by the mighty Aneurin, became the cheer leader, and for the first time that afternoon the crowd showed some signs of life. To judge by the mood both during and after the demonstration the lusty cheers were a flash in the pan, and the coping stone a tombstone in disguise. For, far from putting forward new and far-reaching solutions to the threat of nuclear war, Bevan and the other speakers simply reiterated the decisions of last year's Brighton conference, which called for the ending of H-bomb testing by this country but declined to commit a future Labour government to ban the manufacture or stockpiling of H-bombs unless agreement could be reached by the other nuclear Powers.

To describe, as does the *Manchester Guardian,* last Sunday's meeting an "anti-H-bomb rally" and to refer to Bevan's brilliant and carefully prepared piece of oratory as "an impromptu decision to add to the agenda . . . and make party unity the keynote of his speech" is to our minds the height of political naivety. The composition of the platform, an Unholy Trinity of T.U.C., the leader of the Labour Party and Bevan, the man who, more than any other member of the Party, symbolised (and for some, unfortunately, still does) the forward, uncompromisingly Socialist Movement within the Party, made it quite clear that this was the opening of a campaign not against the H-bomb but with an eye to a General Election in the not too distant future. Recent by-elections have perhaps convinced the Party managers that however unhealthy are the Tory prospects in such an event, the apathy, disillusionment and even cynicism within the ranks of Labour are matters of concern for the Labour politicians who yearn to ride the bandwaggon of power once more.

As farmer Bevan put it: while he had sympathy for those with more distant aims, he felt that, as in 1945, having "sown the harvest, the movement must now collect it". There was, he said, a majority for Labour in the country. So the Labour Party was going to resume some of its traditional activities and organise demonstrations in the country to make clear that Macmillan did not speak for the British people.

But neither can Mr. Bevan and his friends be so sure that the Labour Party "speaks for the British people". Especially when the Party cannot even speak for its members. And last Sunday's demonstration was much less a protest against the Government's foreign policy than it was an attempt to rally the divided forces of Labour by what was, in effect, a not very subtle form of blackmail.

Mr. Bevan's "peroration" which, according to the *Manchester Guardian,* "was as inspired as it was impromptu" consisted in the declaration that

> The time has come for the Labour movement to be united. No more discordant voices. I do not ask for abnegation of thinking. But I ask that action should not be frustrated by theoretical differences. (Cheers). I do honestly believe that the world can be saved from the H-bomb, but not by people who are always looking back over their shoulders at the nineteenth century. The Tories are always looking back to the past glories of the British Empire. I say to them, as I would say to Mr. Khrushchev if he were here on this platform with us to-day 'The days of empire have gone'.

Some of Mr. Bevan's audience may have had difficulty in finding a connecting link between the first half of the "peroration" and the second. What have the Tories' backward glances to do with the frustrating theoretical differences in the Labour Party? Did Mr. Bevan in fact, by a curious slip of the tongue, use "Tories" instead of "Socialists" and "British Empire" for "Socialist movement"? After all, the split in the Labour movement is not simply between jealous and ambitious politicians (supported or opposed, as the case may be, by the vested interests of the Trade Union blocs) but also by that uncomfortable, dissatisfied voice of a conscious minority which by socialism *means* socialism undiluted by considerations of statesmanship or political and electorial opportunism.

When Mr. Bevan referred to those people "who are always looking over their shoulders at the nineteenth century" he was surely not thinking of an anachronistic and dying band of Empire Loyalists but of the obstinate members and outsiders who still believe that Socialism means what it meant to the pioneers of the 19th century, who saw in the organisation of the oppressed toiling masses the weapon for their emancipation and liberation from the shackles of capitalism. Ambitious politicians accept and rely on the rules of the game just as gamblers accept and rely on the laws of probability to "break the bank".

Bevan is a case in point; he is not only one of the most capable parliamentarians, because one of the most knowledgeable of its rules; he is equally, one of the most astute Labour politicians because his whole career is dominated by considerations of tactics and never of principles. Tactics, let us hasten to add, for furthering his political career and not the future of the "class" of which he professes to be a part and in whose interests his political activities are allegedly directed.

This was clearly shown at last Sunday's demonstration. Whilst on the one hand Mr. Tom Driberg, chairman of the Labour Party and of the rally, paid tribute to those who had taken part in the Aldermaston march (why then did the Labour Party not officially support it?), on the other the speeches from the platform were perhaps directed more against the marchers (who for the occasion had rallied, a thousand strong, at Hyde Park and marched to the Square to form a kind of halo around the "solid" Labour phalanx) than against a dithering, backward-looking government.

The Labour and Trade Union leaders are jealous of demonstrations when the initiative does not emanate from Transport House, and suspicious of rank-and-file movements which they cannot control. We have no doubt that the organisers of last Sunday's rally, forewarned that the Aldermaston irregulars had planned to descend on the Square with their imaginative protest of a week earlier behind them, and their slogans held on high, which made the Labour Party's "Ban H-bomb Tests" look more than tame, adjusted their sights and delegated their only orator to deal with these disturbers of the Labour Party peace. If our surmise is correct, then the fact is significant not only as further evidence that the expression of opinion at rank-and-file level is not welcomed even by the Parties which profess to speak for the people, but equally as a reminder to those who might nurture the hope that governments can be influenced in their favour by such spontaneous demonstrations.

At last Sunday's rally, Mr. Driberg proudly told his audience that the march to the Square had been led by Mrs. Floyd, an 86-year-old veteran of the Party. One assumes that Mrs. Floyd was offered to the audience as a symbol (just as the eleven-year-old boy who led the Aldermaston marchers for most of the way was also a symbol) that the Party had not lost faith with the objectives of its pioneers.

Labour has been in office four times — from 1945-1949 absolutely. The Labour Party and the Trade Unions have some nine million members and control large financial resources. They are obviously in a strong position to influence and even to educate public opinion. They profess to believe in Socialism. Only last week, the *News Chronicle* Gallup Survey published a sample opinion on the "burning" topics of this Iron-curtained Nuclear Age which we propose to refer to not because we implicitly trust Dr. Gallup's snoopers or are influenced by a public opinion which is as fickle as the news headlines or a politician, but because in the "democracy" in which we live, it is the only attempt to assess what the people's opinions are at the time on topics of public moment.

According to the Gallup Poll, 44 per cent. of the sample were in favour of Britain and America stopping their H-bomb tests as a result of Russia's announcement that she would, as against 42 in favour of continuing. 61 per cent. disapproved if Britain were to give up her H-bomb "without waiting for America or Russia to move" as against 25 per cent. who were in favour of unilateral H-bomb disarmament. 77 per cent. thought that Summit talks were important and 20 per cent. that they were not.

We welcome, as brothers in the wilderness, the 20 per cent, who have seen through the farce that seeks to impose itself on the public as "vital Summit talks". But what of the 77 per cent., at least a half of whom vote Labour, who believe these talks *are* important? Is this not the most damning indictment of the political, as opposed to the Socialist, approach to the problem of power politics of the Labour Party? Yet this party which addressed the audience last Sunday as "comrades", which through Mrs. Floyd seeks to reaffirm its socialist origins, is knowingly responsible for a "public opinion" professing views which, not only are contrary to its basic interests, but are the denial of the basic tenets of socialism.

Perhaps, after all, old Mrs. Floyd, bless her, *is* the symbol of Labour Party "Socialism". For we forgot to mention earlier that she led their march in a *wheel-chair*.

We see more hope in 11-year-old Roger Kirby who led the Aldermaston protesters. His slender shoulders, and whatever it was that made a young boy prefer the company of a mile of protesting adults to a gang of playmates of his own age, are the perennial guarantee that some, at least, of our youngsters will know how to shrug off the invasive attentions of the politicians and the pressures of the conformists in the years that lie ahead. Their task, however, will be that much easier if we remain true to the values which inspired the founders of socialism.

Looking back over shoulders may be a bad thing for the Grand Moguls of the Labour Party and the Trade Unions. But if in so doing we capture something of the enthusiasm, the determination as well as the uncompromising values and intellectual vitality of those past generations, we may well have a key to happiness, peace and well-being in an age ripe with scientific and technological achievement. War is a symptom, not a cause, of social ill-health; poverty is not the result of under-production but the cause. And happiness? Ah! That is more elusive. But how much less important its final attainment would be if mankind were to free itself from man-made miseries and anxieties with which it is now plagued . . . *quite unnecessarily*.

[April 19, 1958]

EVERYTHING BUT SOCIALISM

The latest move in the top level struggle within the Labour movement is, at the time of writing, a declaration of war on Gaitskell's leadership issued by the executive council of "Victory for Socialism". It charges that during the last few years the Right has had its own way and that under Mr. Gaitskell's "inspiration" it had induced the Party to "muffle the attack on capitalism, play down the radical aims of the party, and choose bi-partisanship with the Conservatives on vital issues, such as the bomb". The impressive *J'accuse* ends with the traditional pat on the back immediately followed by the inevitable slap in the face. Mr. Gaitskell's "personal qualities" may continue for long to be of value to the Labour movement BUT "we believe that his leadership is a source of weakness, confusion and disunity in the party, and that, in the interests of the party, he ought to go".

Mr. Sidney Silverman, one of the seven Labour M.P.s to support the Victory for Socialism declaration, told the Press that he had "admiration" for many of Mr. Gaitskell's qualities "his great intelligence, great ability, great sincerity and very often his great courage. But you cannot be outside right and centre forward of the same team at the same time".

What more generous advance obituary notice could a politician expect to receive from a fellow politician? The only trouble is that Mr. Gaitskell while recognising the dilemma as expressed by Mr. Silverman in football terms, may have as little faith in the outside Lefts of the Party as *they* have in the inside Rights. As we have faith in neither, we can understand the frustration both factions must feel about each other. The Gaitskell inside-rights watch the sands of time running out and the chances of winning elections becoming more remote because of a bunch of agitators whose "image" of the Party, they say, is hopelessly behind the times. The outside-lefts, on the other hand, think they have been a minority within the Party long enough, and realise that they will continue to be so as long as the Party is run by the block votes of the Unions and remains under the influence of the old gang of Labour politicians. Whatever the outside-leftists may say to the contrary, the objective of both factions is to win the next elections.

If the "revisionists" succeed in imposing their plan on the Labour movement, it is almost certain that those of the "purists" who don't change sides will have to start a new party and, at most, hope that they can become a minority force in Parliament with sufficient seats to harass whatever government is in power when it comes to

Divisions. If, on the other hand, the Leftists win the day (which will mean that they have succeeded in capturing the Union block votes, and we don't suppose they will have more scruples about accepting them than Bevan had) then they will be the Party, and the old gang and the Revisionists will probably find themselves seeking to make common cause with a section of the Liberals, who in turn will probably split, with some leaving the Party to join the Tories. Who knows but that within the Tories there may be a minority splitting off to join the Liberals.

Whatever happens things will remain very much as they are now, for at most all we can expect to see happen is the emergence of new political figureheads, the hastening of a process which is taking place all the time on the football field as well as on the floor of the House. Underneath, at the level of the people — and the only level at which social revolutions can take place — the situation will be as it always has been. To change *that* situation requires something more radical than a change of Constitution or a change of Party Leaders. *Tribune* is being its usual demagogic self when it maintains through the pen of Michael *(Marullus)* Foot that the "real cause of the so-called crisis within the Party" is not the "personal arguments and antagonisms which are merely incidental to it", but "the expressions of opinion both within the unions and the constituency parties" which are threatening to oust the hitherto well-established majority represented by the old gang. If this were true surely a socialist wind of change would have by now found expression somewhere, somehow, even in the columns of *Tribune,* for instance?

What is the militant socialism represented by *Tribune?* In the heat of the crisis "Marullus" Foot reminds us 17/6/60 that "*Tribune* is a strong upholder of Parliamentary Government, including the right and duty of M.P.s to exercise their individual judgement and conscience".

Why not for the people as well? In theory M.P.s are the representatives of their constituents; in other words they should represent the viewpoint of the people on the issues under discussion, and this to our minds would be a more democratic expression of the public interest than Mr. Foot's pleading that M.P.s should speak and vote according to their individual consciences, points of view . . . or prejudices.

It is, of course, utter nonsense to suppose that 600-odd M.P.s can represent the interests of 50 million people; it is even more nonsensical, and certainly not socialism, to believe that by giving *carte blanche* to 600-odd M.P.s the interests of the people will either be forwarded or safeguarded. In any case, if that were possible, then there would be no justification for a party system since the selection of candidates would have to be determined by a public examination of their integrity and their superhuman capacity to be the custodians of the nation's interests and conscience. But "Victory for Socialism" dreams of the day when a Labour Party purged of the Revisionists and the old gang will defeat the wicked Tories, and Michael Foot will clean up the Home Office before moving to higher spheres; Ian Mikardo bringing his business experience to the Board of Trade as a start on the road to loftier heights. One can imagine Mr. Zilliacus as Foreign Minister, Mervyn Jones as Minister of Education or Postmaster General, and Sydney Silverman might well be rewarded for so many years in the political wilderness with the job of Solicitor General. And, of course, *Tribune* could become the Official Gazette, edited by Richard Clements and assisted by the *New Left* Boys.

Our facetiousness is not out of place if it underlines the remoteness between the thinking of the so-called Left *élite,* within the Labour movement, and Socialism; between the pretensions of that body to represent true socialism as against the Revisionism of the Right wing. For these "Socialists" there is no contradiction, no antagonism between society and government so long as the government is composed of the right kind of people!

Nearly 200 years ago William Godwin expressed more clearly the distinction between society and government than any of the Socialist thinkers to-day even in their most enlightened moments could dream of doing, when he wrote in his *Political Justice:*

> We should not forget that Government is, abstractedly taken, an evil, a usurpation upon the private judgement and individual conscience of mankind. A fundamental distinction exists between society and government. Men associated at first for the sake of mutual assistance. Society and Government are different in themselves, and have different origins. Society is produced by our wants, and Government by our wickedness. Society is in every state a blessing; Government even in its best state but a necessary evil.

Far from progressing *in ideas* from the times in which Godwin lived, the "Socialist" thinkers of to-day have converted the "necessary evil" of government into a "necessary virtue". The recent publication of Richard Crossman's pamphlet "Labour in the Affluent Society" was hailed by *Tribune* (3/6/60) as "so good, so relevant, so brilliantly written and so devastating a reply to the revisionists that not even a full-page review could do it justice"; and in a full-page review in the *New Statesman* last week, Mr. Bernard Crick describes it as "brilliant" and furnishing "food for thought, or fuel for the flames for many a day". It may well be all that these reviewers say of it. But it is significant that neither of them mentions the word *Socialism* for in fact it discusses everything but socialism, however often it may refer to "fiscal socialism", "socialist government" and to the "socialists" of the Labour Party. Crossman's is not a pamphlet of ideas, nor is it "brilliant" or "devastating", and the "food for thought" consists of two scraps, and even then the conclusions the author draws neutralise their value. On page 5 he writes:

> A Left-Wing Government is required only where the change must be radical and involve a repudiation of orthodoxy; and the occasion for it will be a crisis in which the people, shaken out of its complacency, loses confidence in its traditional rulers and quite deliberately insists that what the country needs are new men and a big step forward.
>
> If this, and not the swing of the pendulum, is the true rhythm of British political development, it follows that the prime function of the Labour Party is to provide an ideology for non-conformist critics of the Establishment, and a political instrument for interests and social groups which are denied justice under the *status quo.* So far from trying to show that its leaders can manage capitalism as competently as the Tories and reshaping itself in the image of the American Democratic Party, the Labour Party, if it is ever to return to power with a mandate from the people, must remain a Socialist challenge to the established order.
>
> A Labour Party of this kind is likely to be out of office for much longer periods than the Tories . . .

To which we would reply that if the Labour Party did its job properly then it would be out of office for all time, for it could only achieve the repudiation of orthodoxy among the people by seeking to create a new sense of responsibility, the success of which could only be measured by the extent to which the people refused to have their lives run for them by a handful of their fellows whether they called themselves Socialists or Tories. Socialists cannot have it both ways. Either they want to foster individual responsibility, in which case they must expect the people they succeed in influencing to refuse to vote for them or anybody else; or they don't believe in the people having a will of their own, in which case let them stop talking about Socialism.

Furthermore, an enlightened people will create their own instruments to express and safeguard their interests. They do not need a political party to be their spokesman. Indeed the moment this happens, the initiative is taken away from the people and all the vices of the political machine will reassert themselves.

The other scrap offered to us by Mr. Crossman appears on page 21:

> A Socialist Government, it is often argued, would be able to finance the huge extensions of welfare, education and other public services to which it is committed by encouraging a much faster rate of development in the private sector of industry and then taxing away a sufficient amount of the profits. This was the policy put forward by the Labour Party at the October election and in the short run any Labour Government would have to attempt it. But experience should have taught us that the run might be very short indeed. In the Affluent Society *no* government is able to give orders to Big Business. After one Budget a Labour Chancellor who tried to squeeze private industry too hard would soon discover that he was not master in his own house . . .

Mr. Crossman's answer to this is that the balance of the economy must be reversed to ensure "that the public dominates over the private sector". By which *he* means that the State and the government must have more and more powers to plan, to regulate the economic life of the country. For Mr. Crossman, then, socialism means more government, more control from the centre. He recognises that such a system gives rise to a State bureaucracy which itself "is one of those concentrations of power which threaten our freedom". And he replies that this dilemma can only be resolved

> by ensuring that the necessary extensions of public ownership should be counterbalanced by expanding the constitutional and judicial safeguards of personal freedom; by reviving Parliament's traditional function of controlling and checking the Executive; and by curbing the oligarchic tendencies both in the trade unions and in the party machines.

But if he fears the threat to freedom of a State bureaucracy which has more and more power, how can he assume *(a)* that it will be possible to expand "constitutional and judicial safeguards" and *(b)* even if this were done on paper, what means would be available to the people to see that these safeguards were respected in fact. By the judiciary? Well, South Africa is the answer to that illusion.

No, it won't work. Socialism must be the means as well as the ends if it is ever to be achieved. Mr. Crossman thinks as a politician and not as a Socialist. His pamphlet is concerned with the East-West power struggle. On economics he is dominated by the achievements of the East bloc; from the point of view of civil liberties he supports the West. And this in broad outline is also the attitude of the so-called Socialist Left, from the *New Statesman, via Tribune* to the *New Left*. These "socialist" intellectuals do not believe in the people. Social changes will come from above. All the people must do is to allow themselves to be used by one set of leaders against those in power. Thereafter their function ceases, except to obey the new rulers.

Socialism, like anarchism, will only be achieved when enough people want it more than the gadgets and tit-bits of the "Affluent Society". This is not an impossible task unless one believes *for one-self* that the material things which are the hall-mark of the "Affluent Society" are more important than freedom, the kind of freedom that stems from the leisure society. Mr. Crossman and his political cronies are obsessed with productivity, finance, unemployment, ownership. These are the values of a capitalist society. Leisure, production for needs, co-operation, are the values of the free society in which there will be room for everybody to expand and live as human beings.

[June 25, 1960]

NAIVE OR OPPORTUNISTIC?

"I did not join this party to become a Leftwing Liberal. I joined this party because I believed that Socialist principles were relevant to the problems of the twenties and thirties and I am more convinced than ever in my life that those principles are relevant to the sixties and seventies... we have to make it crystal clear to the country that there is a fundamental difference in the approach on our part from that of the Tories. There are those who have blurred the vision of our people over the last 12 months or so by suggesting that all we have to do to win victory at the polls is to prove that we can manage things better than the Tories. We ought to be able to do that, comrades; but the real passion of our message which will bring us to victory is to let the nation see clearly that we are aiming at a better and different society from that we have today".

These points are from a speech made by Mr. Ray Gunter, Labour's shadow Minister of Labour, in October, 1960 (at the Labour Party Conference when the unilateralists won their historic card — or paper? — victory). Michael Foot's *Tribune* tells us this week that at the time, it "applauded" these sentiments, and it is to the credit of that journal that it did. We would, however, at the same time suggest that it was either naive or opportunist to "applaud" the utterances of a politician without having serious reservations.

Well, now *Tribune* reaps the harvest, for last week it again quotes Mr. Gunter (two years later, when much dirty water has flowed under the political bridges, and Mr. Gunter has stepped into Mr. — now Lord — Robens' shoes) not with approval but to attack him. At a meeting at Houghton-le-Spring recently he is quoted as saying that:

> One of the underlying causes of our weakness over the past few years has been the absence of any good thinking by the so-called Left. In this crazy world where words seem to have lost their proper meaning, the so-called 'Left' is in reality the most reactionary 'Right'. Instead of the 'Left' being forward-looking, vigorous and irreverent, they relentlessly combat change — they shout old war-cries — nostalgic for old battlefields. *Tribune* always seems to me to fit in very nicely with days around Queen Victoria's Diamond Jubilee.

And poor old *Tribune* quoting chapter and verse from the socialist bible and from our Ray of 1960 shows that he is wrong and they are right. So long as they talk about socialism, of course they are right. The moment they engage in party and power politics Gunter is right and *Tribune* is "Victorian" as well as, in our opinion, dishonest. Forget about Gunter, and think of the *Tribune's* "God that failed":

Nye Bevan. Is it not doubly significant that he "failed" the movement when he was the Opposition's shadow Foreign Minister (assuming that history will declare that he served it when he was Health Minister in the 1945 Labour Cabinet). For at his famous pro-British-H-bomb speech he was defending two basic principles of parliamentary (and power) politics: that force is the basic "argument" of executive government, that in international politics might is right, as well as being considered the only respectable approach so far as the electorate was concerned.

Of course Bevan was not a "bad" man, any more than Gunter is the conscious turn-coat *Tribune* makes him out to be. He, like Bevan at the time, wants his party to be in office, and, of course, wants to enjoy the sensation of power, of being a *real* and not just a *shadow* Minister. And to this end it is essential to create a monolithic party, one which will have popular appeal among an electorate brain-washed by mass-communications, the advertisers and the "market-researchers". In order not to have to periodically point an accusing finger at the "gods-that-fail", *Tribune* and *Peace News* should try to live *without* gods (human or supernatural). They would perhaps spend less column-inches and time building up personalities, which in due course they would have to destroy, and at the same time concentrate their propaganda on developing ideas, the validity of which depends on their possible application to human problems and aspirations. To link ideas to particular individuals invites, rightly, in our opinion, the objection that what is advocated is possible only for and by a minority, an *elite* but nor for and by ordinary mortals.

[May 19, 1962]

3
The Trades Unions or The Dog that Wags the Party Tail

NO INDUSTRIAL PEACE

When asked, many years ago, what the Labour movement wanted, Samuel Gompers, the New York cigar maker who founded the American Federation of Labour in 1881 (and was its president until his death 44 years later!), replied in one word: "More". "The answer remains the same", writes George Meany*, president of the A.F.L. in 1955. "Our goals as trade-unionists are modest. We do not seek to recast American society. We do seek an ever-rising standard of living — by which we mean not only more money but more leisure and a richer cultural life". As to how they will get "more" Mr. Meany pins his faith on "voluntary collective bargaining" which he says can exist

> only in the environment of political freedom . . . And so we are dedicated to freedom, not only political but also economic, through a system of private enterprise. We believe in the American profit system, in free competition . . . Collective bargaining is not a means of seeking a voice in management. We do not want so-called "co-determination" — the representation of unions on the board of directors or in the active management of any company.

Mr. Meany forecasts that in the next twenty-five years — in this age of automation — a thirty-hour working week will be sufficient to

*In *Fortune,* (New York, March 1955)

provide the standards he demands for the workers, but ends with these words:

> Advances in technology alone do not solve the great social problems. These are questions not of science but of wisdom. I feel that the voluntary co-operation of labor and management in a free society can carry us far toward their solution.

In an article in *Forward* on "What do we Mean by Equality", Hugh Gaitskell, former Labour Chancellor of the Exchequer and strongly tipped as one of Attlee's possible successors, writes:

> As for exploiting there are certainly many Socialists who still feel that it is wrong that a man should make a "profit" out of employing another. But frankly, in these days of powerful trade unions and full employment the mere fact of employment in private industry does not excite much moral indignation . . . The emphasis in British Socialist thought and propaganda has shifted away from the idea that private ownership of the means of production as such is utterly wrong, and towards the notion that it is inequality not related to merit or function which is the real trouble.

"Equality", wrote Mr. Gaitskell earlier in his article, does not mean identical incomes or uniform habits and tastes. What he means instead by equality is

> a classless society — one in which the relations between all people are similar to those hitherto existing within one social class; one in which though there are differences between individuals, there are no attitudes of superiority or inferiority between groups; one in which although some are paid more than others, the differentials are based on generally accepted criteria — skill, responsibility, effort, danger, dirt, etc.; one in which though people develop differently, there is equal opportunity for all to develop.

At the congress of the Confédération Générale du Travail (C.G.T. — the communist dominated French Workers' General Confederation representing a majority of organised workers) held in Paris last week, an overwhelming majority of the delegates accepted the secretary general's report that "progressive pauperization" is inevitable as long as the capitalist system survives, against the minority view which argued that an energetic and constructive trade union programme can do something to improve the workers' lot.

One cannot explain away the diametrically opposing views expressed by the A.F.L. and C.G.T. spokesmen simply by dismissing the latter on the grounds that being communist dominated it must be "politically" inspired and divorced from reality (any more than one can discount the validity of the campaign of the E.T.U. (Electrical Trades Union) for shorter working hours launched at its conference last month on the grounds that its president is a communist). One must instead seek the reasons, and accept one or the other, since both cannot be correct estimations of the situation in the basic approach to the relationships between workers and employers (or management).

In countries such as the United States and Britain "a new managerial class has arisen on both sides of industry" — as Viscount Woolton so succinctly expressed it in the House of Lords last week, the result of which is the maintenance of the *status quo,* with capitalism dressed-up in a bowler hat, a Montague Burton suit and a pair of boots (not forgetting the presentation watch and chain for long and devoted service).*

In countries such as France, Italy and Spain with their tradition of struggle, where a recognition that the day to day struggles of organised labour are simply a means of survival and defence against the abuses of the employing class and not an end, in these countries the idea still persists, even among thinking intellectuals, that fundamentally there can be no reconciliation between the contrasting interests of workers and employers.

The French writer, Raymond Aron, in a much discussed book just published in Paris**lists the six *griéfs fondamentaux* (basic grievances) of the worker as follows: 1. Insufficiency of remuneration; 2. excessive working hours; 3. threat of total or partial unemployment; 4. discomfort associated with the technical or administrative organisation in the factory; 5. the feeling of being imprisoned in the *condition ouvrière* without prospects of advancement; 6. awareness of being the victim of a fundamental injustice by reason of the fact that he does not benefit from the national product and that he is denied all participation in the direction of the economy.

Mr. Meany for the A.F.L. believes that "collective bargaining" will

* The Conservative Minister of Labour, Sir Walter Monckton, addressing the general conference of the International Labour Organisation in Geneva (June 17) said, on the question of human relations in industry: "One thing is certain, the carrot and the stick can no longer be regarded as the only driving forces on which industry should rely . . . The conditions of freedom and dignity which we demanded for everyone in the Declaration of Philadelphia must be recognized as applying in the work place just as much as outside it. We must understand that a man brings more to a factory than the work of his hands. He brings a part of his life — he lives it there — and he should be able to enjoy rights and satisfactions in that working life just as he does in his life as a citizen. The study of those rights and satisfactions and the most effective means of securing them should be a major task of the I.L.O. in the years ahead."

** l'Opium des Intellectuals (Calmann-Levy, 1955)

provide workers with a solution to the first four of these "basic grievances" so long as they repress the fifth and sixth. Mr. Gaitskell, for British "Socialism" more or less discounts the last two "grievances" as being of no consequence (who but a Labour Party politician would accept Mr. Gaitskell's definition of a "classless society" in which there is "private ownership of the means of production" and differentials?). But this is the fundamental mistake both trade union leadership and management make. They seek "peace" in industry through collective bargaining, wage tribunals and conciliation boards as if these methods of determining social and economic differentials will ever expunge the humiliating injustice of the exploitation of man by man. Indeed, if ever such a situation should exist then the workers of the world will have not achieved the status of free men but deserved the badge of slavery.

[June 25, 1955]

AUTOMATION AND THE WORKERS

Anarchists perhaps tend to be over-optimistic in their appraisal of the potentialities of certain trends and developments in society. Yet it seems to us that the giant strides made by science in this century and its application to the techniques of production — for Man's destruction as well as for a better understanding of his "nature" and behaviour — could lead to his complete enslavement or liberation; this revolution in science cannot, we submit, take place beneficially to mankind unless there is a corresponding revolution in our social thinking. At the time of the recent elections none of the Party managers thought it expedient to tackle the question and make an issue of it. But now that this all-important matter for the politicians has been settled, and their jobs are unquestioned for another five years, some of the real issues, some of the "facts of life" can be ventilated more freely. As for the recent strikes, they have been much more valuable perhaps in this direction than the narrow issues over which they arose. For Press and Parliament at the moment, the topic of the day is Industrial Relations.

"Never at any time this century have the broadest groups of people been so well-off" maintains the *Daily Express* and the question so far as they are concerned is to know "what then has gone wrong". The logic of the question is quite clear, because these supporters of capitalism and Empire take for granted that everybody accepts as an absolute truth that society will always be divided into rulers and ruled, directors and workers; into those who lead and the many who follow. Such an assumption might have been made a century ago with some degree of confidence, but to-day the complexity of industrial production and organisation is such that without a skilled and intelligent work force it would be impossible for the industrial machine to function. Modern capitalism, therefore, is faced on the one hand with the need for raising the standard of education, of health and of life in order to ensure maximum productivity, and on the other with the social problems that the raising of these standards creates.

At present perhaps the greatest stress is placed on advancement as measured by money. But at some stage in this struggle a point will be reached where, all industries having their wage scales linked to the cost of living, every increase in wages will be automatically nullified by an increase in the cost-of-living index. One imagines that the capitalists, supported by the Trade Union bosses, will declare that only increased productivity will produce higher standards for the workers. In fact, already to-day, there is a growing awareness among workers that their improved standard of living is due to working longer hours (not to mention the contribution made to the family budget by the wife's earnings, which in many cases becomes an indispensable source of income) and not the result of a growing economic egalitarianism in society. The demand for maintaining, or even improving, living standards whilst at the same time working shorter hours will prove to be a much more far-reaching demand in a positive direction than differentials which serve to consolidate capitalism rather than weaken it.

To our minds capitalism is in retreat not so much as a result of pressures from the Trade Unions (indeed, the president of the National Union of Vehicle Builders, speaking at his Union's annual conference, recognised that for many socialists the policies of the Labour Party are "helping to give capitalism a new lease of life"), but as a result of its own internal problems. Crises used to be resolved by means — including wars — which would, if applied to-day, create as many new problems for capitalism as they had solved. But it is a fighting retreat in which capitalism seeks to save that which is fundamental to its continued existence — the *social* differential. By aiming at giving everybody a stake in society — as the Prime Minister put it recently: "to spread property ownership widely instead of merely destroying private prosperity" — the ruling classes hope to remove certain deep-seated class antagonisms without removing the differentials which exist to-day, not only among railway workers, but among the "property owning" section of the community as well.

To this end, the tactic of capitalism is to absorb the Trade Union movement. The slogan will be the over-riding interest of "national prosperity" which demands the closest collaboration between the employers and an organised, responsible, working class.

Such a role is far from distasteful to the Trade Union leadership. Their acceptance of invitations to talk things over with the new Prime Minister at Downing Street; their openly declared confidence in the Tory Minister of Labour (indeed, in so far as such appraisals are relative, is Sir Walter Monkton any worse than *their* late lamented Ernie Bevin?); their support of wage freezes and their efforts to extend controls over the working community — all are clear indications of the lines along which the T.U.C. leadership is thinking. But such attitudes are also indicative of its own internal difficulties, and we think these are not far to seek. Hitherto the "unity" of the Trade Union movement was assured by the greedy and reactionary attitude of the employing class and the stark reality of a large army of unemployed workers — rarely by a positive ideal. Working conditions, hours of work and wages, have, so far as the principal industries are concerned, ceased to be matters over which a direct struggle between worker and employer takes place on the spot. To-day they are legislated for at some remote "high level" for the country as a whole, and for all workers whether organised in a Union or not. Unemployment as a technique for increasing production has lost its attraction for most industrialists who are as much, if not more, concerned with the problem of markets for their goods than with productivity; and a prosperous internal market requires full employment (of the womenfolk as well), and even overtime.

Thus viewed, capitalism has removed the props on which trade union unity was supported. And in spite of all the talk of "human relations" in industry, of the workers having their "share of the cake", the deep cleavage in society persists.

We were reminded of the ideological ossification of Trade Unionism by an article in the *Manchester Guardian* (June 22) recalling that it is a hundred years since the last of the experiments in Owenite co-operative socialism came to an end. The Leeds redemption Society, as the last survivor was called, and which was founded in 1845 to enable "the Working Classes to work out their own Redemption by Union among themselves", published a monthly paper, the motto of which proclaimed the goal of the new society as — "Labouring Capitalists, not Labourers and Capitalists". One can, at a distance of a hundred years, smile at the naivety of these Redemptionists whose motto "Labouring Capitalists" was in fact a contradiction in terms, but the terrible reality is that the objectives of present day Trade Unionism are the same in spite of a century of experience. And what is even worse is that, intellectually at least, the Tories of 1955 have caught up with the Redemptionists of 1855 . . . and the Trade Union bosses of 1955 in this country and America.

It would be, unrealistic however, as well as sectarian to write off the Trade Unions because their objective has been a limited one, though when their obituary comes to be written we feel that no one will deny that they outlived their welcome in that they retarded the development of the social revolution. In any case it was not our intention to hold a post-mortem on Trade Unionism but rather to look forward to this coming age of atomic energy and automation, which is no pipedream but a fact.

In a society not divided by classes, the advent of atomic energy in industry, and the robot factory, would be welcomed by all as triumphs of technology for reducing the problem of providing the basic needs to proportions which would allow to all the necessary leisure to concentrate on the much more important problem of living full and interesting lives. But that is not the reaction to-day. At the Conference on Automation held in Margate last month it was quite clear that Industry is only interested in Automation as its predecessors were in the automatic loom and the steam-engine: that is, how industry can benefit *financially* from its application.

Labour for its part views Automation not without suspicion: will it create unemployment they ask, and the Trade Union leaders express themselves as being content if they can have guarantees that Automation will not result in a lowering of living standards in the industries where it is applied or in a large number of workers having to sign on at the Labour Exchange because they have become "redundant".

From the point of view of the community, indeed of mankind as a whole, the attitude of Industry to Automation is narrow and inhuman; that of the Trade Unions, defeatist.

All the appeals to "human relations" in industry exuded by the Government and its supporters in last week's Commons debate on Industrial Relations were simply a means to an end, a seeking after a *modus vivendi* between Labour and Capital so that the existing economic system might survive (whatever *they* may say, capitalism without the co-operation of workers cannot operate; we have yet to have proof that mankind cannot survive without capitalism). What of the Trade Union Leaders? Has their struggle also become a means to an end? Are we in fact witnessing a struggle for *power* between the managers of industry and the managers of Labour? Such an hypothesis, we think, could be substantiated by drawing parallels between the relations of management to industry and of T.U. leaders to membership, the unquestioning acceptance by the T.U.C. of the existing economic system, and their remoteness from, and general hostility to, their membership. But the fact remains, irrespective of the validity of our hypothesis, that Trade Union leadership can offer very little to the workers in the industrial revolution confronting them. Just as this revolution brings with it new techniques, a new psychology and a new vocabulary, so must the workers' movement be infused by a new outlook, new objectives and also a new vocabulary. At the very least those who produce the cake should be in the position to determine how it shall be divided. At best the cake could be large enough for all to help themselves according to their needs.

It is here that our anarchist optimism manifests itself, for, to our minds, atomic energy and automation provide us with the key to a world of plenty in which working hours and dangerous and unpleasant work will be reduced to a minimum. And to those who might say: "But atomic energy is also the key to the Hydrogen bomb, and Automation the door to mass unemployment" we can only reply that it is our ability to think and reason that distinguishes us from animals, that gives us the power to love or to hate . . . which provides us with the powers of choice. But we must repeat our opening remarks: the industrial revolution of our time demands also a revolution in thinking. It will not come from the Managers of Industry and the Trade Union Leaders who stake their future in the social structure of the past, but from the "dispossessed" who can well afford to forget the past and cast their glances into the future and its potential store of well-being and happiness.

[July 2, 1955]

COMPETITION OR CO-OPERATION

It is a curious phenomenon that whenever a major industrial stoppage seems certain, Fleet Street and the politicians suddenly discover that but for it, prosperity is awaiting us just round the corner. As the *News Chronicle* put it last Monday:

> All the evidence encourages the belief that if we could solve our industrial problems and clear away restrictionism, all the old fears of unemployment and bankruptcy would disappear. The fault is in ourselves, at least in those among us who put prejudice before patriotism and prosperity.

The Minister of Transport and Civil Aviation added his irrelevancies when he told a meeting at Sunderland last week that:

> There has been a lot of talk about the position of our shipbuilding industry. The country should know the facts. In the last three months all over the world, new orders for tankers to the extent of no less than 8,000,000 tons have been placed. Out of this vast total Britain has only secured 700,000 tons of orders. In other words, we have not secured a tenth of recent orders that have been placed.
>
> That is one of the reasons why I hope that the industry, both sides of it, will take the honourable and sensible course and take advantage of the means of settling this dispute which is open to it.

Apart from the fact that we can see no relation between the 10 per cent. of orders for tankers placed during the past three months and a strike that started this week, surely this is not an unfair proportion, especially since we are also told that British shipyards have £900 millions in contracts and are fully booked up with work until 1961.

But these are just the conscious, superficial scare tactics turned on on such occasions to drive a wedge between the public and the strikers. What we find more disconcerting, and dangerous, are the assumptions made by both sides in regard to the relationship between Capital, Labour, the State and the Community, and it is these considerations which we propose to discuss.

Trade unionism came into being as a weapon for defending and furthering the interests of the "working classes". These interests range from improved working and safety conditions to shorter working hours and higher pay. They include what are called restrictive practices, closed shops and annual holidays. They do not, however, in any way question the fundamental relationship between employer and employee. They recognise that though the workers make the industrial cake it belongs by right to the boss. Their only grievance, when they have a grievance, is that their share of the cake is not large enough. We think it important to stress what is an obvious fact, because it is just the obvious which in times of industrial unrest gets lost in a fog of patriotic platitudes, economic clap-trap and journalistic witch-hunting.

Because their objectives are what they are, the official Trade Unions are militant in times of "prosperity" and impotent in periods of "trade slumps". It is also significant that it was during the wars of 1914-18, 1939-45 that they found greatest official favour. And it was during "slump" periods that not only membership fell off and T.U. power was curbed, but that the growth of militant, unofficial rank-and-file movements took place. (It is in the years immediately preceding the first world war that we see the emergence of social theories such as Syndicalism and Guild Socialism which were not concerned so much with a fair share of the cake but in actually controlling how it was to be made and distributed. The war of 1914 saved the Trade Union leaders' skins as well as that of the employers).

Apart from the exceptions that prove the rule, the growth of Trade Unionism in this country has been motivated less by workers' solidarity than by sectional economic interests within the working class itself. In spite of the eventual organisation of unskilled labour in the late '80's, the Trade Union movement to this day remains segregationist — not only *racially* and *nationally,* as only too clearly demonstrated in these post-war years, but also so far as *skills* are concerned. By creating, or encouraging, "classes" within a class the Trade Union leaders have weakened the movement both in the economic field as a collective bargaining instrument, and in preventing its ideological development. With the passing of the years Trade Unions have moved always more to the Right, towards reaction. This reaction — even after taking into account such positive trends as represented by the Shop Stewards movement, or the attempts at creating breakaway organisations — deeply influenced the attitude of the workers themselves both towards their Unions as well as on a personal level. That the sharp drop in membership of the Trade Unions during trade slumps in the inter-war period was a reflection of the impotence of the Unions, is, we think, only part of the explanation. It is after all when the struggle is hardest that one would expect workers to make common cause with their fellow victims, but instead only too often has their attitude been one of "each man for himself".

However much as anarchists we deplore this attitude, it does not surprise us. But the national Press and the political leaders do not deplore this attitude in principle, but are surprised and shocked when it manifests itself in reality. The Liberal *News Chronicle* which has been of late plugging the ideas of free enterprise, competition and differentials, declares that:

> It is difficult to make any calm comment on the strike news to-day. Any sensible person must feel sickened by the silliness of the struggle. Both the unions and the employers had strong arguments to back their original claims, but their attitude has made the dispute a squalid exhibition of stupidity and sectional prejudice.

The *Manchester Guardian* whilst recognising the rights of bosses and workers to bring industry to a standstill declares: ". . . Responsible men will go to extreme lengths only when some great issue of principle is at stake. What is the issue here? It is simply a dispute over money . . ."

"Simply a dispute over money", that mere bagatelle which divides society into the "haves" and the "have-nots"; which prevents one half of mankind from obtaining the food it needs to live; which makes it possible, to quote the *Manchester Guardian* again, for a "handful of angry and injudicious men who control the working lives of some three and a half million wage-earners" to bring a large part of manufacturing industry to a standstill within a week if "they have their way".

It would be interesting to know what "great issue of principle" would, in the opinion of the *M.G.,* justify workers — and employers presumably? — going to "extreme lengths". We are also curious to know why the *News Chronicle* refers to the "silliness of the struggle". The bosses who have the cake are resisting attempts by the workers to have a bigger piece of it. From our point of view they may be silly for allowing the bosses to have the cake at all, but why should *liberals,* of all people, complain at such undignified squabbles?

The Trades Disputes Act of 1906 makes a strike or a lock-out a legal act. The Liberal and Tory upholders of free enterprise are obviously in a difficult position, for as believers in the sanctity of the Law they cannot but recognise the rights of workers to withold their labour and employers to close their factories if they so wish. And, being believers in free enterprise, they must encourage competition between workers as well as between employers. But at the same time they demand that both employers and employees should act in a responsible way to the community as a whole. They raise their hands in horror when the secretary of the Boilermakers Union declares that the interests of the country come second to those of his members, or when a spokesman for the Engineering *employers* makes it clear that:

This time, we don't want Government interference. This is quite positive. We want to fight it out ourselves. We have to stand firm and prove to these fellows that things are not done so easily.

"Responsibility to the community" implies a oneness with one's fellow beings which can only be achieved through co-operation and mutual aid. Competition, classes and differentials are the antithesis of co-operation. But these are the values which regulate human relations and behaviour to-day. Let us not be afraid to admit that they are the values not only of employers but of a large section of the workers too.

We cannot hope, or expect, that the section of the community which thinks itself superior to the rest of society and accordingly deserving of material and social advantages, will abdicate its positions of power and privilege for the sake of the well-being of the community which it despises and exploits. But can the "under-privileged" majority do no better than try to ape them?

[March 23, 1957]

MOVEMENT WITHOUT IDEAS

Addressing the conference of the Civil Service Clerical Association in Britain last week, the secretary of the TUC, Mr. George Woodcock, pointed out that collective political activity by the trade unions was both necessary and inevitable and that no limit need be placed upon it so long as two conditions were met: "the unions should speak with a united voice and their answer to any problem must be based on their industrial experience and responsibility". And on the grounds that

> if we can in one way or another reflect a common view we can have a tremendous influence in this country. But a fundamental condition of our authority as a trade union movement is agreement. If we cannot get agreement we can do nothing

Mr. Woodcock argued that the movement should decide on one of two things:

> that we shall generally come to a common agreement in the interests of our members and in the light of our industrial experience; or that we shall leave alone matters on which people differ irreconcilably.

Even support for the Labour Party by the Trade Union movement, said Mr. Woodcock, was based on "industrial experience". Clearly, for Mr. Woodcock such matters as unilateral disarmament are worthy of discussion by the movement only if there is the prospect of unanimity of opinion for or against. But where there is a deep division of opinion "then I begin to wonder," he said, "whether we can continue to be involved in discussion of this kind".

Of course one can see what Mr. Woodcock means. There is no point in having behind one a mass movement to underline an arguement or a demand if, in fact, there is more than one arguement or many demands which betray a division of interests within the mass movement. But to imply, as we think the general secretary does, that it is only the political issues which divide the movement, is to gloss over the fundamental weakness of Trade Unionism in this country which, by its craft division, is anything but a homogeneous, united, mass movement. When Mr. Woodcock talks of coming to "a common agreement in the interests of our members and in the light of our industrial experience", he is expressing sentiments which have no connection with reality.

Like the Common Market and EFTA, the Trade Union movement is all at sixes and sevens for not even workers in the same industry are united let alone as a class. And, furthermore, there is not a single political or industrial issue which can be settled except at the expense of some section of the community's "interests". Take the burning topic of unilateral disarmament as an example of a political issue. If it were to come about tens of thousands of workers (including scientists and technicians) in the best paid jobs going to-day would be looking for other employment, possibly having to move into other districts and having to accept a lowering of their living standards. Many of these people will be inclined to allow their personal, immediate "interests" to colour their judgment as to what is the best interest of the community of which they too are members.

It may also be recalled that the workers in the Woolwich Arsenal, and in the naval dockyards at Chatham, were incensed when the Government's "new look" armaments programme relegated these establishments to the scrap heap. From the point of view of the community it was a good thing (or at least it did no harm). But to those employed in these establishments it appeared that their world was crumbling around them.

Again, the replacement of coal by oil is a matter which a united community should welcome, because no feeling and thinking person can take for granted that fellow beings should have to spend their working lives underground and in constant danger, when alternative and more easily accessible sources of power are available in sufficient quantities to satisfy all our needs. But for the miners, oil is a threat to their "jobs" and the workers engaged in the oil industry are no less their enemies than are the Shell and Standard Oil empires. But not only is there division among Trade Unionists as a result of new industries ousting old ones, but there is, also, divison within branches of the same industry based on a concept of classes within the working class. Railway employees for instance belong to a number of different unions depending on the kind of work they do, (it is true that the NUR accepts all grades), and in recent years one has had to witness the miserable spectacle of disputes, based on inter-union rivalry, as bitter and determined as any they have ever waged against the employers.

It seems to us that there can never be "agreement" in the Labour movement so long as workers in the same industry are members of different unions as well as being party to a system of financial differentials which inevitably raise social barriers and encourage petty rivalries between the workers themselves. A workers movement which seeks to remove the social and economic injustices of capitalism cannot succeed by, at the same time, encouraging differentials — financial and social inequalities — among its own members. Every human being has the same need of the necessities of life irrespective of his individual capacities; the fact that some people are more gifted than others, far from being a justification for their enjoying higher material standards of life should, if anything, be a strong reason for limiting them in view of the intellectual resources they can draw on to enjoy a full life. Instead the trend not only of the employers (which is understandable) but of the Labour movement (which in view of its leadership is also understandable, but inadmissible) is to encourage and reward the more resourceful members of society and penalise those who for one reason or another, generally beyond their control, lack the skill, adaptability or resources needed to be "successful".

The weakness of the Labour movement is of course that it aims at abolishing neither the capitalist system not the privileged society. Or to put in another way: the trouble with the Labour movement is that it does not believe in Socialism! At the annual conference of the Transport Salaried Staffs Association last week, Mr. Ray Gunter, M.P. (remember him? He was a Labour "discovery" either at Scarborough or at Blackpool last year) in his presidential address said:

> Brilliant and modern executives are too often excluded because their connections are not "quite right". Above all else this nation needs leadership — dynamic and adventurous . . . politicians, trade unionists, and business men should search their souls and move from a past that is in so many aspects irrelevant, on to the challenge of a new and unexplored era.

In the foregoing remarks is summarized the official Labour movement's twisted concept of the classless society and Socialism. What these people want is equality of opportunity for members of all classes to join the privileged class. Not for them the abolition of differentials, or the £24,000 per annum Dr. Beechings. What they demand is that everybody should have a chance to join the rat race. And then they are in favour of the rat race!

But why do these Gunters expect that the underprivileged members of society should "prepare eagerly for the coming of automation" when all they can see in it is the spectre of unemployment and more privileges for those at the top? And what kind of "progress" was he talking about when he declared that "it was something of a tragedy that at this moment of acceleration in man's progress a dreadful apathy seemed to be on the British people".

At Southport the Executive of the Boilermakers' Society was fixing "January 1963 as the last month in which it will tolerate a working week of more than 40 hours".

And they talk of "progress". With something like seven out of ten women working in jobs outside the home as well as their men, plus all the discoveries of science and the new technology, it is still "not possible" to enjoy the 40-hour week which was being advocated by workers' organisations more than seventy years ago!

We shall be told that the working man now has, besides the necessities of life, a Telly, a Car and a Fridge which were never dreamed of by the pioneers of the '80's. That is true, but it's not these gadgets which prevent us from enjoying a shorter working week. It's the production of all the things we don't need (beginning with the "defence" programme), and the so-called "services" which keep thousands of people "gainfully employed" and provide profits for those who employ them, but which are of no public use (beginning with the advertising industry), which ensure that there will be no reduction in the working week so long as the capitalist system of production prevails.

Unlike Mr. Gunter we are not looking for the way to give rein to the "brilliant and modern executives". What we need more than ever to-day is that just a modicum of public *common sense* should be tacked on to the brilliant discoveries of science and technology. The common sense which will ensure that production shall be geared to needs, and the discoveries of science used to reduce to a minimum the hours of work to maintain life, so that we may all have the leisure to live.

[June 10, 1961]

'STREAMLINING' THE UNIONS?

Though Mr. Harold Wilson as fraternal spokesman for the Labour Party at the recent Blackpool Congress of the Trade Union movement, was careful to point out that, of course, "you have to deal with whatever government is in power", the tameness of the debates, the absence of controversial "political" issues, and the good press all this earned, indicate that the T.U. bosses had their eyes on the next general elections, and that while they have to "deal with whatever government is in power" they reckon to get a better deal out of a Labour Government. As to whether their members will be any better off under one government or another is doubtful. Mr. R.H.S. Crossman, M.P., in his *Guardian* column declares that

> This year's Trades Union Congress seems to me the best thing that has happened to the Labour Party for a very long time. The decisions it has taken are already making the kind of impact on public opinion that should help us to turn anti-Tory into Labour votes at the next election.
>
> Even more important, these decisions could, if they are followed up, enable a Gaitskell government to introduce the real, centralised Socialist planning which was impossible in 1945 owing to the attitude of the trade unions to wages policy.

Mr. Crossman goes on to argue that until this year's Blackpool TUC the Labour Party's close association with the trade unions has been an electoral liability.

> Just after the last election some of my colleagues became so worried about our image as a working-class trade union party that there was even a suggestion of dropping the name "Labour" as well as Clause 4. Even from a pure vote-getting point of view, the idea was ludicrous. Images aren't things you can put on and take off at will. An image is merely the impression you make on other people, and the only sure way I know of effacing a bad impression is by changing the behaviour that caused it. But one of the things a Labour Party in opposition cannot do anything about is trade union behaviour. Our trade union connections were bound to remain an electoral liability until the trade union movement woke up, took a look at itself, saw what was wrong and decided to put it right.

And thanks to Granada Television millionaire-socialist Sidney Bernstein's decision to televise the Blackpool congress, the impression, the image, that the public has of the Trade Union movement has been changed overnight. "The Tewson epoch has ended; the Woodcock epoch has begun!", and Mr. Crossman has already started counting the votes which "could be worth 50 seats to the Labour Party"...

There were three major issues debated at the Congress. Firstly there was the motion of the Union of Postal Workers asking the TUC General Council to inquire into the possibility of reorganising the structure both of the TUC and the British Trade Union movement. For a number of different and sometimes contradictory reasons delegates were almost unanimous in supporting this motion. Mr. Bob Edwards, who is an enthusiastic supporter of the Common Market, thought "a modern structure" was needed if British trade unionists "were to hold their own in the Councils of Europe", while Mr. Shanley wanted the reorganisation in order the better to challenge, and not to support, the Common Market. Other delegates saw reorganisation as a means for showing "a united front on such problems as unemployment, technical change, redundancy, wages and hours". The Postal Workers' delegate, opening the debate, considered that

> We ought to be looking at ourselves to see whether our organisation can be streamlined to meet changes in industry and improve the impact and force of our organisation. The structure of the trade union movement is secondary to the policy of the trade union movement.
>
> If we are serious about the possibility of greater unity, we should each be able to say that our organisation was in the melting pot with others and that all should be willing to examine the possibility of reorganisation and make a contribution to it.

The fact that to-day only half the male workers and a quarter of women in jobs belong to a Union was in itself a challenge to the Unions. But what does this streamlining of the Unions mean so far as the Trade Union bosses are concerned? Of course the Trade Union movement needs reorganising if it is to challenge effectively the injustices, the inequalities, and the maldistribution of wealth that prevail in capitalist society. Workers can only speak with one voice when they have a common purpose. The present structure of the Trade Union movement creates more inter-union rivalry, more struggles between workers, than militancy against the bosses. But is it militancy against the bosses, and governments, that the Union leaders are seeking to encourage by their proposals for streamlining the Unions? Mr. Woodcock's remarks should make it clear that the new "image" of the T.U. is anything but revolutionary:

> Resisting the temptation to go into the subject too deeply, he saw the purpose and structure of the trade unions reflecting the time when governments were indifferent to economic welfare, "and certainly to the welfare of working people". He conceded they might still be indifferent to an extent,

but it was also true that they were not likely now to have a Government which would decline to accept responsibility for promoting economic health.

Secondly, the Congress debated the Common Market and defeated by 5,845,000 bloc votes to 2,000,000 a motion opposing British membership and calling for a general election before the "decisive" step is taken. It approved the General Council's own report; the critics called it a "fence-sitting" report, the Economic Committee preferred to describe it as keeping the door open!

Thirdly they debated Wages Policy. Again this debate was dominated by Mr. Woodcock who made two significant remarks:

> We must not, as a trade union movement, give the impression that we are claiming absolute, unfettered, unqualified freedom to do whatever we like, and to hell with everyone else. That is not trade unionism.

He also defined the task of a modern society thus: "To find the practical limits of regulation we could all adhere to". This, he said, was what the Government had never attempted, and he added:

> "We are not a bunch of crate eggs on wages. We have never shirked our responsibilities. We will respond to decency. We have had lots more experience than the present Government and I wish one of these days the Government would really begin to listen to the TUC instead of trying to make us the scapegoat for its own failures".
>
> Even if a central agreed objective was established, Mr. Woodcock argued, the TUC would be subject to the same limitations as the Government. Asking himself what the TUC could then do he replied: "I don't know. I can see what the Government cannot see, that it is not so easy to move on this matter."
>
> Union sovereignty could not be sacrificed, and there could be no final control of wages. A discussion in which the TUC took part could not lead to anything like the pay pause or the guiding light. One could not have that sort of wages policy. At the most one could induce a mood of a sense of responsibility.
>
> "Our problem is the same as the Government's. We have no power to direct our affiliated unions as the Government has tried to direct us. We must move with the only instruments we have — reason, argument, and an appeal to the solidarity of the working people."
>
> Thus, the Government had two theoretical alternatives: It could try to impose restraint on working people by law and force — although he doubted if it would succeed in this — or, it could seek to create responsible attitudes which would respond to sensible, fair, reasonable and responsible stimuli.

Maybe Mr. Woodcock's and the General Council's problems are "the same as the government's" and the sooner the workers wake up to the fact, the sooner will *they* themselves decide to reorganise their unions to serve their real interests. Common Markets, Wages Policies, are concerned with maintaining financial stability, balancing budgets, and preserving the unequal society. "Organised Labour" to-day should be thinking of how to reorganise production and distribution to satisfy the needs of everybody. The means of production exist, the technical know-how too; the needs of the people could easily be ascertained and we have the "labour power" to produce these needs. That is the task of the people in our "modern society". And there is no longer the excuse that there isn't enough to go round. If we stop producing useless things like armaments, and discourage waste, there is not only enough for everybody in the developed countries; we should be making a start in helping the people of the under-developed countries to enjoy similar prosperity.

But the Trades Union Congress at Blackpool last week, however it proposes to reorganise, and streamline; whatever it has done about its "image" and its vote catching potential for the Labour Party, made it quite clear that it remains a pillar of capitalism. "The Tewson epoch has ended" but to our minds the "Woodcock epoch" which has begun is if anything more dangerous. Mr. Woodcock, as well as being an ambitious politician, is also an intelligent one. Under those bushy eyebrows lurks a determined bureaucrat, behind the quiet, unemotional voice, a mind made up. Workers beware!

[September 15, 1962]

TRADE UNIONISM BY TORT

What with the doctors' strike in Belgium, and all kinds of token strikes in the public services in France and Italy, not to mention go-slows among the postal workers in this country, and the recent threat of a power stoppage, the Trade Unions are in the news everywhere. And the forces that would seek to curtail what they consider to be their excessive powers are also expressing themselves in no uncertain manner; and not only the employers, but the Press as well as the so-called representatives of the workers.

A Trade Union is described as "an organised association of workmen of a trade formed for protection and promotion of common interests"and though one knows that less than a century ago it often needed courageous and determined men to undertake to promote these common interests, and in many parts of the world this is still true, the fact is that to-day, in a country such as Britain, trade unionism, as defined, is an anachronism and the Trade Unions, are a conservative and reactionary organisation.

A writer in the *Guardian* last week*, discussing the P.E.P. pamphlet by John Cotton on "Trade Unions and the Law", describes the Trades Disputes Act of 1906 as "an outstandingly brave piece of social legislation by a great Liberal Government", for, it

> deliberately set out to be inequitable, to tilt in favour of trade unions the scales of that even-handed law which as Anatole France put it 'with magnificent impartiality forbids both rich and poor alike to sleep under bridges and to beg for bread'... The Act of 1906 laid down that trade unions could not be sued for alleged torts (roughly, civil misdoings like breach of contract which are actionable in normal circumstances) committed during trade disputes. That is still the law, and it gives trade unions a unique position in society over a wide field of activity...*

Apart from serious modifications to this Act by the Act of 1927 following the General Strike of 1926 (which shows the relative protection offered by the law) and which the Labour Government in the flush of victory repealed in 1946, it is ironical that the only other serious challenge to this Act of 1906 should have come from an ex-Union member on the grounds of victimisation. We do not propose to deal in detail with the *Rookes v. Barnard and others* case which has been engaging the attention of lawyers these past eight years, though the issues involved deserve to be mentioned as relevant to the points we are attempting to make.

*Fair Shares at Law, by J.L.R. Anderson *(Guardian)*

Douglas Rookes was a draughtsman employed by BOAC at London Airport who in 1955 resigned from his union, the Draughtsmen and Allied Technicians Association. He is described as a political radical — incidentally, in his row with the Union's paid organiser (a Communist) over his resignation, the latter described him as "a traitor, a blackleg and an anarchist" — and was his Union's representative on the airport's Local Joint Panel as well as a member of the Union committee in his own office. His resignation came "as a result of a process of disillusionment which exploded when he thought the union was more interested in politics than in improving working conditions". The Union retaliated by threatening to come out on strike if BOAC continued to employ him. BOAC acceded to the Union's threat and Mr. Rookes was sacked. That was in November, 1955 and it has taken eight years for the lawyers to unravel the legal implications and for the House of Lords to give a decision in favour of Mr. Rookes.

The Lords decision was that the strike was unlawful on the grounds that there was a joint agreement that there should be no strikes or lock-outs and that the union official involved was not protected by the Trades Disputes Act. The interpretation in both the Press of the Left and of the Right is that the Lords decision seriously affects the right to strike. Yet it seems to us that the Lords decision in favour of Mr. Rookes is based on the grounds that in threatening to strike if he were not dismissed by BOAC the Union concerned was in breach of the contract it had made not to strike (or not to strike without giving six months' notice). And unlike the *Guardian* writer who defined a tort (the Act of 1906 refers to "any tortuous act") as "civil misdoings *like* breach of contract" (our italics), G.D.H. Cole in a footnote in his *Short History of the British Working Class Movement* defines a tort as "in effect, any civil wrong (as distinct from a criminal act) *other* than breach of contract" (our italics). And to further clarify the issue we quote from a "Dictionary of Legal Terms" in *Everyman's Own Lawyer* where a tort is defined as

> An injury or wrong suffered by one person at the hands of another, *irrespective of any contract between them:* but distinguished from a crime as not being a wrong done to the community as well as to an individual, and hence not punishable under the criminal law. (Our italics)

No wonder it has taken the lawyers eight years to make up their minds what Section 4 of the Trades Disputes Act of 1906 actually means! The Lords decision does not seem, as a lawyer is reported in *Tribune* (January 31) as saying, to put "the whole right to strike . . . at issue". In any case, assuming this were to be the case it would only mean that such was the law, and as everybody knows, even if they are reluctant to admit it, what progress mankind has made is the result of enough responsible and courageous people being prepared to break the law. After all, Trade Unions were frequently persecuted and suppressed by law in the past in the very countries where laws to-day exist recognising the rights of workers to organise. (Sticklers for the law may be surprised to learn that it was only as recently as 1935 that the Law in the United States recognised these rights).

The *Rookes v. Barnard* case does, however, raise the question of the right of every individual to secure a job whether he belongs to a union or not. Where organised workers are weak they cannot prevent non-organised workers from accepting inferior wage rates and bad conditions and from threatening their standards. Where they are strong they can surely afford to be magnanimous to non-union workers and seek to win them over by demonstrating the advantages that can be achieved through unity. A union which contracts with the employer not to strike or be locked out but which is prepared to strike in order to deprive a fellow worker of his livelihood for having committed the abominable crime of resigning from the union, is surely not worthy of our sympathy, *whoever the individual concerned may be.*

If trade unionism is not to be equated with free-masonry, or monopoly, then one must assume that trade unionists recognise that the individual acting alone is weak but in concert with other individuals of like mind is strong. But we also assume that he needs power in order to fight power (the boss class) and not to browbeat the weak (the unorganised, the individualist, worker). But, obviously, one cannot in the 60's make such assumptions and not expect to be accused of utopianism or just simplicism. Yet who is naive? — the anarchists who, to-day echoing and confirming Bakunin when, nearly a century ago, he declared that "the only way . . . is complete solidarity in the struggle of workers against the employers" or the Labour-Party-enthusiasts who to this day believe their mission as spokesmen of the Trade Unions (after all, the TUC *et alia* gave birth to the Party in 1906) is to legislate for the emancipation of the working classes?

The anarchists have failed to bring about anarchism just as the social democrats have failed in their attempts to introduce socialism, but with this very significant difference: that whereas anarchists have never ceased to point out that anarchism will never be achieved by authoritarian means, socialists have insisted that the classless, libertarian society could be attained by the ballot box, by government, by States which "wither away" and pave the way for the state of affairs which we call anarchy. And socialists, since the Russian Revolution, have had countless occasions to put their theories into practice. After two world wars they have had mass opinion behind them; and they have been swept into office only to reveal themselves more concerned with playing the political game, according to the bourgeois-capitalist rules, than with legislating the privileged class out of power. In Britain, for instance, a Labour Party with an overwhelming majority and sustained by a political mood (after more than five years of war and promises by the politicians of pie-in-the-sky as the fruits of the defeat of Hitlerism) which bordered, even here, on revolution, gave birth to what? . . . another Labour government in 1950 with an unworkable majority which led to new elections in 1951 and the overwhelming victory of Churchill and the Tory party!

After thirteen years, during which the ruling class have enjoyed an administration run by the hunting and shooting fraternity, the prospects are that the public's crosses will return the *friends of the people* that is the Labour Party.

What does this mean? It is true that the Stock Exchange, expecting a Labour Party victory at the polls, has welcomed the Prime Minister's announcement that elections won't take place until the Autumn, and the optimist might well refer to this as proof that a Labour victory will upset the employers. But market prices are upset and revived by the most bizarre events at home and abroad. What is much more significant in the context of our argument is the statement, made only last week, by Sir John Hunter to the British Employers' Confederation in his last speech as president. He was urging leading employers to prepare themselves to co-operate with a Labour Government and to be ready to do so without being forced to under the threat of legislation. He told the Confederation meeting that they had studied the legislation Labour have promised to introduce, which "covers improved social benefits and insurance contributions; industrial relations and questions such as redundancy pay; industrial safety and health" and

Such a programme will mean many new calls on employers' time and money. But I do not subscribe to the view that a Labour Government will introduce legislation with little regard for employers' views.

On the contrary, I believe a Labour government will listen attentively to the views expressed by employers' organisations — on one condition: that those views are positive and expressed clearly, forcibly and without reservation.

A heavy burden will therefor lie on us to crystallise our own thinking on a number of difficult subjects.

Sir John went on to point out that "as in the past we shall have to oppose many Government and trade union proposals" he did not expect opposition to be "very effective" unless it were accompanied by "positive and constructive alternative proposals". He even rebuked some members for "waiting to see what the Government are going to do". Such an approach is realistic but hardly that of a group or class particularly concerned whether the government calls itself Tory or Labour. While a Labour government could *hardly refuse* to introduce some legislation which a Tory government could *hardly agree* to introduce (without the contenders for your votes being completely indistinguishable and obliging you to vote for Mr. Khrushchev or Sir Oswald) it is surely quite clear from the statement by the retiring President of the Employers' Confederation that his members have nothing to fear from a Labour victory — which they expect — at the coming elections. The fact is that the Trades Union Congress is the dog that wags the Labour Party tail. And the TUC is in no mood to introduce Socialism. For a large number of people (and we humbly bow to, and exclude, the "enthusiasts" who are wedded to a cause and who devote much of their leisure time to it) Trade Unionism is an onerous job which they carry out, however, with no more feeling of vocation than the man whose job it is to sell bricks or detergents.

[April 18, 1964]

GREAT FUTURE FOR CONTENTED COWS

Tory and Labour M.P.s view the Budget with despondency and elation respectively — their immediate concern being votes at the October General Election. According to the *Guardian* City Comment (April 15): "The City is delighted with the Budget. The general view last night was that the market will open better today". And Mr. George Woodcock, the general secretary of the TUC, was reported by the same journal as "welcoming" the budget as "courageous" though he thought it 'lacking in inspiration'. We are told that Mr. Maudling has "taken a gamble on savings and taken back in taxation about £100 millions, no more than the TUC — or Mr. Woodcock at least — considered appropriate".

The *Guardian's* Labour correspondent goes on to suggest that

> on the more constructive part of the Budget — if it has one — neither side of industry can claim that much heed has been paid to its usual pre-Budget entreaties, the promised White Paper on a corporation tax is in line with TUC thinking, but there was no shifting of the burden of taxation on the grounds of greater social justice, for which the TUC stands.

We concluded the article, *Trade Unionism by Tort* on a cynical note because, in our opinion, Trade Unionism in this country to-day is part and parcel of the capitalist system. George Woodcock and his fellow "directors" sell Labour just as Mr. Bloom sells washing machines and holidays in Bulgaria and in the process both put over *their* "personalities".

In a sense Bloom is more "human" than Woodcock. He sells mass-produced machines and treats them as commodities, whereas Woodcock seeks to manoeuvre human beings as if they were commodities and, like Bloom, charges for them according to their performance.

There are anarchists who argue that it is unrealistic to expect the Trade Unions to be what they were never intended to be. Even if we limit ourselves to that definition which states the function of the Trade Unions to be "an organised association of workmen of a trade formed for protection and promotion of common interests" what reason is there to assume that these "common interests" must inevitably always be the same. To write off the Trade Unions as reactionary and conservative bodies *per se* ignores the fact as pointed out by the Webbs in their *History of Trade Unionism* that they have "at various dates during the past century at any rate, frequently had aspirations towards a revolutionary change in social and economic relations". Are the Trade Unions to-day pillars of capitalism because of their structure and leadership, or are they what they are because the membership is what it is? Is the Trade Union movement reactionary because its members are concerned with improving their economic situation regardless of questions of social status and human dignity? If this is the case, anarchists it seems to us, can help to reverse the trend, not by seeking to draw away the revolutionary elements from the workers' movement, and thus leaving it even more at the mercy of the professional negotiators (while achieving very little with a revolutionary organisation which represents an infinitesimal section of the working class), but by working within the Unions as anarchists, supporting the day to day demands for improved working conditions and a larger slice of the cake of production, and at the same time using every opportunity that presents itself to underline the ephemeral nature of legalistic methods of wage increases so long as the people do not control the means of production, the land, and all the sources of natural wealth.

Less than half the working community in Britain belongs to a Trade Union. It is true that among the 58 per cent. outside the Unions are individuals who are militants and who either have a "conscientious objection" to belonging or are not eligible, but let us be realistic and recognise that we shall find more revolutionaries among the "organised" 42 per cent. than among the other 58 per cent, apart from the fact that eight million organised workers are much more a *potential* force against the status quo than eleven million non-union workers.

Anarchists have a more important part to play in the Trade Unions to-day than ever before — at least so far as the affluent nations of the West are concerned. For if the Trade Unions have become, as it were, part of the Establishment it is because the "prosperity" of the working class is as much the concern of the ruling class as it is of the Trade Union leadership. As one Trade Union apologist for the "closed shop" pointed out in a BBC programme the other night, many employers "welcome" it — that is 100 per cent. trade unionism — obviously because they then know where they stand, and are not involved in struggles between the workers themselves. At the same time we read of Union leaders who oppose limitation of Company profits on the grounds that it is against the interests — the "prosperity" of the workers!* It seems to us that such a chaotic situation is a golden opportunity to drive home to the workers the

*A view shared by G.D.H. Cole

anarchist arguments which expose and transcend the petty interests both of boss and "boss's man".

The *raison d'etre* of capitalism is, as ever, production for profit. The giant strides made in the field of technology during World War II in the interests of "bigger and better" destruction could not suddenly be turned off like a tap when Man eventually stopped slaughtering Man, and the problem which has faced the industrialists in the post-war years has been that of productive potential outstripping purchasing power on a scale undreamed of in the pre-1914 or the inter-war years. In an effort to expand markets for the industrial nations all kinds of financial expedients have been resorted to; at home it is Hire Purchase facilities, and for the have-not countries long term loans and "aid". But this is not a new solution. Britain was doing just this in the 19th century, and just as the long term effect was to create, as Cole puts it, "powerful rivals to the British producer . . . and bitter rivals in the remaining markets of the world", so the industrial development of the undeveloped countries to-day can only be viewed as a stop-gap solution to the problem which, if anything, will blow up on a much bigger scale than ever in the not too distant future.

The industrialists and their economic "experts" are obviously aware of what is building up. We believe they have discarded war as either a solution or even a regulator, whatever they may think of the effectiveness of a cold-war economy. And because, in this writer's opinion, financiers, industrialists and politicians no less than CNDers, Committee of 100 and anarchists, want to go on living, an H-bomb war has been discarded because the destruction of mankind — capitalists, politicians and indutrialists included — does not *solve* the problems of capitalism.

What, then, are the kinds of solutions one may expect in the next fifty years under a capitalist system? We foresee an intensification of monopoly on an international scale in order to streamline production of specific commodities to levels which have a relation to "demand" (industrialists denounce *nationalisation* but have no objection to take-overs, Common Markets and other monopolistic measures and set-ups. Where's the difference? Is it not significant that a Dr. Beeching is as much at home as boss of a nationalised industry as he was as boss of Imperial Chemicals Industry?) We also foresee that workers will enjoy greater purchasing power, will work fewer hours (with new industries thriving on the exploitation of leisure) and that the unemployed, the aged and other unemployable members of society will have a New Deal. All that the Trade Unions of the past struggled to achieve for their members will be done by the employers' corporations automatically, not out of love for workers, but in the interest of profits and the maintenance of privileges. The only snag in this utopia of contented cows will be that though everybody in the West has all the gadgets, the services and the time-consuming pastimes that man's ingenuity can think up, the world will be suffering from a chronic shortage of food. Or will capitalists have found by then how to make food production as profitable as the manufacture of useless gadgetry?

We have attempted to present a picture of the Capitalist future because we believe that only by seeking to foresee what our rulers have in store for us and concentrating our propaganda on the real dangers, can our efforts be used to their best advantage. And this applies with added force to the Trade Union movement which has the power, if only the rank and file could be made conscious of it, to halt the trends we have outlined — or at least those which will result in the concentration and consolidation of Power, economic and political, in huge international combines — and seek to direct the great discoveries, the "breakthroughs", in the fields of science and technology towards satisfying the basic needs of all mankind.

[April 26, 1964]

TAKE THE INITIATIVE!

A correspondent in last week's *Freedom* commenting on the editorial "Contented Cows" could not see of what use was our suggestion that anarchist should urge workers to demand wage increases and improved conditions if, as we also suggested, modern capitalism in its own interests would be obliged to encourage prosperity among the workers anyway. Apart from the fact that we were attempting to observe long-term trends, (which does not blind us, however, to the present situation, which is that basic wage rates for most workers are sufficient only to provide the bare necessities of life), we do not believe that it is either the function or in the interests of wage earners ever to leave the initiative to the boss, and therefore however willing the boss may be to increase the workers' purchasing power, their demands should always be for more than he is prepared to concede.

There can be no permanent *modus vivendi* between labour and capital if only for the reason that the relationship is one-sided: because power is onesided. Trade Union leaders and politicians have a vested interest in inequality among men, and it is therefore not surprising that while they agitate for equality of opportunity they also fervently believe in the maintenance of differentials. Everybody, they declare, "should have the same opportunity of getting to the top". But as everyone knows, it is not possible for everybody to get to the top, and therefore the "equality of opportunity" which they champion means, at most, that ability and not wealth or nepotism should be the criterion in determining who will belong to the new privileged class. But every privileged class seeks to perpetuate itself, and so even if we succeeded in having a ruling hierarchy of brains one can only assume that they would be even worse tyrants than their predecessors since they would use their brains as well as brute force (police, laws, armed forces) to consolidate their power.

If, then, equality of opportunity is to be more than just a means for creating a new privileged class, a new inequality, or a meaningless slogan, it must involve not only a revolution in the educational system but also a revolutionary assault on the existing ownership and distribution of wealth of every kind. The nationalisation of the land, mineral wealth and the means of production with full compensation, which is the socialists' alternative to individual ownership as at present, could lead to a planned production in which considerations of need, and not profits, were paramount, but it would not end privilege, and the present power of the employers would be transferred to the State. There is enough evidence around us to convince any thinking person that the State as an employer can be a harder task master than the individual employer.

If wage earners are not to jump out of the frying pan of free-for-all capitalism into the fire of State capitalism or, which is just as bad, resign themselves to spending a working lifetime in the frying pan, they must be convinced in their own minds that a practical alternative exists which will make their lives richer, freer, more meaningful and satisfying in all respects. Anarchism is the alternative; we have no doubt about that. Our doubts, and most of the discussions among anarchists, are centred on how to put over our propaganda so that it convinces an ever larger number of people, more than intellectually, of the need for a revolutionary upheaval of established values; and, equally important, that anarchist means would, in the event, be adequate to have a reasonable chance of succeeding.

In trying to discover the best means to propagate anarchist ideas we anarchists would be more effective if we learned to relate the importance of anarchism as a guide to our ways of life as convinced anarchists, to the preoccupation which most people have with the symbols of status, security and success.

Our correspondent whose letter we referred to earlier, having argued that our suggestion that anarchists should urge workers to demand more would be "playing into the capitalists' hands", offers his alternative which is that

> Perhaps the only realistic programme for anarchists is that of 'contracting out' of capitalism. For 'contented cows' (your vision) do not make revolutions. Individuals with values other than the materialism of the herd can, however, make their own private ones.

Apart from disagreeing with the contention that his programme is "realistic" we must also point out that in the editorial on "Contented Cows" we were concerned with seeing how the limited resources of anarchist propaganda could be most effectively harnessed in view of capitalist trends which are determined, we hasten to add, not by the capitalists' love of mankind but by the current problems of production of their own making, the result of *their* disunity and greed. The probable "only realistic programme" offered by our correspondent is a programme *for* anarchists whereas our concern as anarchist propaganists is not to advise anarchists how to run their lives, because we assume that they can deal with this problem for themselves, but how to communicate anarchist ideas to non-anarchists.

If we are told that our propaganda should be linked to our personal experience our reply would be that if we believed it were possible for *everybody* to live as anarchists in the existing set-up then it would be dishonest of us to oppose the existing set-up and our propaganda should be directed to making people aware of its potentialities. We oppose authoritarian society with every argument at our command because we are convinced that if a limited number of individuals with intelligence or wealth can get-by in society as it is, that is live their lives to the full by reason of their intelligence and/or wealth, they do so only because the overwhelming majority are cut off, for one reason or another, from both. To attract more people to our ideas we must talk to them in a language they understand; that is, we must, in expounding our ideas convince people we are human, understanding beings, who share their problems, and persuade them that it is *because* and not *in spite of* these problems that we believe in the validity of anarchism.

Our correspondent in his proposed "programme" cuts the Gordian knot just as do the socialists when they plump for "equality of opportunity". Both run away from the problem which is how to do away with the system which makes it possible for man to exploit man. Our correspondent by "contracting out" of society, or socialists who fondly imagine that they can graft equality on the rootstock of capitalism by calling it "equality of opportunity", do nothing to disturb a system rooted in privilege.

For those of us who wish neither to escape from, nor dominate, mankind; who want to be themselves *in* society and do not inhabit some ideal island of the imagination, the world around us is vital to our enjoyment of life, and we are propagandists *because* humanity matters to us. To "contract out of capitalism" in a capitalist society means, if one carries out one's threat, living a hermit's life, and most anarchists, to our knowledge, enjoy life and the company of their fellow beings, perhaps more than most people.

Anarchists are "bad" propagandists, compared with the Marxists, for instance, because since by definition anarchism is the denial of authority, and propaganda can so easily be interpreted as imposition, many anarchists look upon propaganda as an "immoral act". Yet progress, in the best sense, is the assimilation of ideas and knowledge, which fertilises more ideas and leads to further discoveries which in turn are handed on to the next generation. Propaganda, for us, is simply our contribution to furthering — and hastening, we hope, — a general recognition of anarchist values.

There are a hundred and one ways of making anarchist propaganda; every convinced anarchist just by expressing his ideas to others at every available opportunity furthers the cause of anarchism. And far from suggesting that we and our readers should all "contract out" of capitalism we would urge all those of you for whom anarchism means something more important than an intellectual concept, to communicate *your* "discovery" not only to your family circle, and your close friends, but far and wide. Propaganda is one form of communications which can brainwash or enlighten. Anarchist propaganda aims at making people think for themselves and not of persuading them to let others think for them. If only for this reason it deserves your support!

[May 3, 1964]

4
The Means: Elections & Vote-Catching

THE MYTH OF 'GOOD' GOVERNMENT

The socialist advocates of "good" government as a practical and progressive alternative to "bad" government must surely admit that their theory that government can ever be anything but "bad" is receiving one set-back after the other these days. Their arguments for the "good" government theory are that while recognising that it is not an ideal form of social organisation nevertheless, if only we could put good men with good ideas at the helm of the ship of State all would be well. The trouble to-day is that we are governed by "bad" men and equally "bad ideas".

Even if we forget the bad old pre-war years; close our eyes to the lessons to be learned from the revolutionary government of Russia or the Popular Front governments of France and Spain, and limit ourselves to a survey of these post-war years of "liberation" from the yoke of fascism and colonialism, is there honestly any evidence to support this "good government" theory? Israel, the brand new State, born of the persecution of a people for their minority (rather than their religious) status; India, liberated from humiliation and the rule of the pukka sahib by a resistance movement which made imperial government untenable; Ghana granted its independence through a combination of circumstances . . . in these countries, leading the governments are "good" men; not cheapjack professional politicians, but men who paid for their resistance with long terms of imprisonment. Educated men, men who, we are told, much more enjoy browsing in Blackwell's Oxford bookshop or spending their evenings with old friends than shouldering the burdens of State. Has their background as "good" men, as intellectuals, in any way made their governments "good" governments?

Perhaps, to answer this question, one needs to define the objectives of "good" government? Is it the raising of the standard of living or that of the nation to the status of a world power? Is a good government the one that succeeds in maintaining law and order . . . or a combination of all these? We are hard put to think of other "objectives", yet in considering the above list we cannot point to *any* government whose objectives were in fact the *lowering* of the standard of living, of *reducing* the nation to that of a third rate power, or of *abolishing* law and order.

All governments hope for the acquiescence of the people just as they all surround themselves with the necessary force to impose their wishes should that acquiescence be absent. All governments respect the "rule of law", a meaningless phrase since it is the government which makes the laws, and breaks them, to suit its convenience.

The fact that to many of us the difference between the regimes in Spain and Russia and those in the "democratic" countries is tangible should not, however, lead us to confuse a subjective reaction with what should be an objective appraisal of government *per se*. It is surely significant that totalitarian regimes arise in those countries where existing governments have lost or are on the point of losing control for a number of reasons: either as a result of popular discontent or from rebellion within their own ranks (generally among the hierarchy of the armed forces). Hitler, Mussolini and Lenin are not phenomena of particular countries. They can arise in any country in similar circumstances. In this context it is worth quoting Winston Churchill's 1935 summing up of Hitler:

> One may dislike Hitler's system and yet admire his patriotic achievement. If our country were defeated I hope we should find a champion as admirable to restore our courage and lead us back to our place among the nations.

Hitler's "patriotic achievement" was in fact to restore the power and prestige of government in a country in which previous governments were powerless to maintain "order" or solve the economic and political problems of the hour. Which of these governments was "good" and which "bad"? By Churchill's 1935 statement it is clear that he thought Hitler's government *good,* however much he disliked his "system", and the Bruening government, which had no power, *bad.* On the other hand, if one accepts Jefferson's view that "That government is best which governs least" then the definitions could be reversed.

The fallacy of attempting to divide governments into *bad* and *good* is surely exposed in the foregoing. Governments survive not because they are good or bad but because they are *strong*. Governments are strong in so far as there is a general public acceptance of the *principle* of government. They are weak where the resistance to government — not the particular government but the system itself — is strong. Thus it is those countries in which a revolutionary situation is present which are also the potential victims of dictatorial government. It is obvious that this should be so. But reformist socialists dishonestly argue against revolution (and for "good government") on the grounds that revolution *inevitably* breeds dictatorship, which is in fact not true. The man who attempts to scale a mountain may well slip and be killed; but he may also reach the top. The man who forever stands at the bottom is sure not to slip and break his neck; neither, however, will he ever reach the top of the mountain!

The advocates of "good" government are either wishful-thinkers or politicians, and both believe in ruling elites of "good" men, in spite of the fact that Machiavelli warned us in *The Prince*, more than 400 years ago, that "a ruler must learn to be other than good". And men like Nkrumah, Ben Gurion and Nehru in our time have confirmed the wisdom of these words.

[August 7, 1957]

THREE PARTIES IN SEARCH OF VOTES

The "silly season", as Fleet Street calls the holiday months, is over: the new political "term" has started with three Party conferences in quick succession. As we write, the Labour Party at Brighton is (according to the *Evening Standard)* "lashing out" against the Government and the Prime Minister (who has been described by Mr. Harold Wilson as "a great bookmaker turned pawnbroker"), just as the Conservatives will, a week or two later at their conference, praise the Premier and "lash out" at the dangers of Labour in office. Preceding the conferences of the Big Two, was the desperate voice of Liberalism from the beaches of Southport attacking both Tory and Labour and proclaiming the need to "split the vote if this means you will unite the country". Obviously only liberalism can unite the country!

While warning his audience of the dangers of electioneering, "The two major parties would get more and more absorbed with their chance of office, and pay less and less attention to the country's problems", the Leader of the Liberals, Mr. Grimond, got so carried away that he was quite unaware of the fact that his own speech was no more than a forceful piece of party peptalk, unequalled even by Mr. Harold Wilson on the opening day of the Labour Party conference. But it is not surprising. The Liberals under Mr. Grimond are desperate men and women.

> "We have passed the point of no return. The old lifebuoys which have kept this party afloat so long are dropping astern, and in the next ten years it is a question of 'Get on or get out', and let us make it 'get on' ".

It was no use for Liberals to try to liberalise the Conservatives or denationalise the Labourites; a kind of "brains trust standing on the side-lines shouting advice to Tories and Socialists alike". Mr. Grimond was, in fact, not prepared to lead a "party of eunuchs or a party which had foresworn direct political action". And his final peroration was directed to those people "who wanted to keep their hands clean of politics"; from angry young men and women, up to the professional classes and business management.

> Too many of them, he said, were simply the Pontius Pilates of modern life, quite ready to criticise but not willing to take the ugly decisions and take the blame for them. But the situation was too serious for anyone to stand on the side-lines. He believed that if political confidence could be restored for the future, there was nothing which could not be cured in the country's economy.

What, we wonder, are the "ugly decisions" Mr. Grimond and his angry young men would have to take if in office? Opposing "socialist solutions" — it was "partnership the workers required in industry, not nationalisation" — as well as the Conservatives' ineffectualness in keeping in check the cost of living, Mr. Grimond plumped for a bit of Socialist controls and a bit of Conservative free-for-all (and the devil . . . ?) as the Liberal approach:

> If the situation got desperate controls might be unavoidable for a very short while, but Liberals would oppose their reimposition except in the direst need, because production would be retarded and inflation not cured but merely turned into new channels.

Clearly this is not a policy but political tactics, indicative of the way the Liberals would muddle through. (After all, the Tories do not believe in controls until the situation created by the financiers forces them to curb their activities "for a very short while"). If anything Mr. Grimond said in his speech was significant it was surely the following:

> the temper of a Government was even more important than its practical proposals, and it was this which had been lacking over the last six years. Only those who thought the random strokes of a chimpanzee created great art could possibly believe the spasmodic intervention of the Governments since the war added up to a policy.

If we understand him aright, by "the temper of a Government" he means the determination with which it governs. Not *less government* for the bogus heirs of radicalism but *more government;* not *spasmodic* intervention but presumably *a firm hand;* not a *laissez faire* economy with workers and bosses happy partners, but firm political control. We can sympathise with the Labour Party man who cannot make sense out of this approach, but then neither do we believe that an electioneering speech ever makes much sense when transferred to the cold columns of print. In the atmosphere of the Conference Hall, aided by loud-speakers and delegates yearning for a cocktail of hope and inspiration, Mr. Grimond's criticisms of the Big Two were substitutes for a policy, and his quips (amplified) the roar of defiance by the "people" against "the arrogance of the two major parties". How heartening that "The vote belongs to the people not to any political party" must have sounded in that little world of liberals!

What have the Liberals got that the other two between them haven't? What have they to offer the people that the others haven't already tried out? Even Mr. Grimond doesn't really know why the

Liberals should be preferred to the other two parties. At least it is what this extract from the report of his speech sounds like to us:

> The Liberal party could not carry the day but it was a nucleus. Its policies might require to be further developed but that would come very rapidly if it could reach the position of being the alternative. He was not interested in how many seats they were going to fight — they had 150 candidates at the moment — but they would fight as many as the country demanded.

Isn't Mr. Grimond putting the cart before the horse; of wanting to be the "alternative" first and then developing the policies after? Or is it not a confirmation of the validity of the questions we have just asked, and that the Liberals are banking on being returned to power on a wave of public disgust for the other two parties?

No political party or organisation however left-of-centre it may be can present itself to the public with a "policy" which clearly differentiates it from any other party or organisation, so long as it proposes to implement its policies through the existing State and governmental machinery. Truer still, we believe, is this assertion when the existing economic and financial set-up is the basis of these policies. In such circumstances policies may perhaps differ in details which the party propagandists magnify into "an issue" at election time, but viewed objectively they only serve to underline the common ground which makes the change of government a no more serious interruption in the daily life of a country than the death of a king or president. In saying this we do not underestimate the influence such "details" of policy have on the elector when it comes to voting. This does not disprove our argument, it only strengthens it. For, it means that a swing in the votes is brought about by details and not on basic differences between the parties.

It is widely conceded that if there were a general election to-morrow Labour would win. This foregone conclusion is based (apart from the general assumption that a change of government might be for the good — though objectively there is no reason why it should not be for the worse) on the Rent Bill introduced by the present government which hits more people than it favours among those who voted Conservative, and which the Labour Party proposes to amend if it is returned at the next Elections. Important as this issue is in the day to day problems of our lives it is surely a proof of the superficiality of the public's approach to life itself and to the individual's understanding of self-interest when an election can be decided over an issue such as the Rent Bill.

To Labour's vote-catching Ace, Lord Hailsham could well reply for the Tories with the Joker of tax-free overtime and sixpence off the price of cigarettes, and thereby create a real dilemma for millions of electors which could only be resolved by calculations to determine which Party best represented the "people's interests". And on this basis the public preference for one party might be decided by a saving of a few shillings per family per annum.

We are not trying to be facetious though we admit to not being able to take these Party conferences seriously. They remind us of the market place in which three eloquent salesmen are trying to talk us into believing that the very ordinary tin of baked beans each is offering is really the most exquisite *Haricots blancs à la Maître-d'Hôtel, Cassoulet de Toulouse* and *Haricots rouges à l'Étuvée* respectively.

We might be forgiven for being seduced by the salesman's eloquence and the colourful labels, into sampling not one but all three tins. But to go on, conference after conference, election after election trying their tins and expecting them to contain anything but baked beans (red, white or green) does not invite forgiveness but makes the examination of one's brains imperative!

[October 5, 1957]

SELF-INTEREST AND VOTING

The pattern of voting in the recent General Election was, so the political analysts tell us, determined by what the electorate considered to be its *self-interest*. It's all very well for those who complain that it was the vote for "self-interest" that won the elections for the Tories, but do they imagine that a large proportion of the Labour Party's twelve million votes was not obtained for the same reasons? Indeed, Labour increased its representation in those areas where unemployment is above the national average, or where certain industries are on their way out and the livelihood of workers and shopkeepers is threatened.

The Labour Party were just unlucky in not being in a position to choose the date of the election But just as they would have made it coincide with the trade recession and growing unemployment, and a Suez or Nyasaland crisis for good measure, Mr. Macmillan who as leader of the government alone determines when the date shall be, naturally waited for the recession to temporarily recede, and the Suez stench to be smothered by the sweet smell of his Moscow Peace Mission, before letting loose the quinquennial political free-for-all. And why not? It's playing the game according to the rules, and if the Labour Party consider them unfair, why didn't they do something about changing them in 1945 when they were in office with an overwhelming majority (almost double that of the present Government)?

A correspondent asks us: "When will you get it into your heads that apathy and self-interest in politics brings a de Gaulle nearer and anarchism yet further away?" Surely such a question is not meant for us but for the leaders of the Labour Party. Self-interest as we understand it presupposes a very active interest in what is going on around us; how else can we know where our *real* self-interest lies? We don't get excited about "politics" for three weeks every five years; it is part of our daily lives, influencing our relationships and contacts and informing our attitudes and values. Apathy, *superficial* self-interest, nationalism, racialism, ruthlessness in human relations, envy and material insatiability, these are the products of party politics. Little wonder that most anarchist and *honest* socialists refuse to become embroiled in the party game even when one of the contestants for office offers such tit-bits as Nyasaland for the Nyasas, utopia for the old and playgounds for the young.

The basic fact still not realised in spite of our much-vaunted literacy, our mass-communications and our "political democracy" is that what shapes economic and social life to-day is not the political party in office *but the system which they administer.* That system is capitalism, and during the five years in which the Labour Party were in office with an absolute majority, they made no attempt (or if they did, then the fact that nothing was changed would indicate that they had no real power — a sobering reflection, surely, for those socialists who advocate the social revolution via the ballot box) to change that system which was designed to perpetuate all the economic and social injustices of a class-ridden society. They attempted to round off a few rough edges of the unequal society, they nationalised a number of industries and public services, handsomely compensating former shareholders (how many of them now vote Labour?), and to convince everybody that no assault on the System was intended, declared that nationalised enterprises must "pay their way", a direct hint to the workers concerned that for them the change was only one of masters; they were still employees, and as insecure in their dependence on the decisions of Boards as they were formerly under the bosses. How ironical the objectives of the Labour Party (set out in 1918 and still standing, more or less) must sound to the miners in 1959 as they receive their "cards" from the Board:

> To secure for the workers by hand or by brain the full fruits of their industry and the most equitable distribution thereof that may be possible, upon the basis of the common ownership of the means of production, distribution and exchange, and the best obtainable system of popular administration and control of each industry or service.

(Perhaps the fact that it is Sir Fred Bowman, *ex-miner* chairman of the Coal Board, who gives them their cards and not some equally titled *former-mineowner* makes all the difference . . . at least for the Labour Party).

When the Labour Party was formed in 1906 its basis was a very simple one, and eleven years later it was still: "to organise and maintain in Parliament and the country a political Labour Party". Only in 1918 the Party, according to Mr. Attlee (now globe-trotting *Lord* Attlee) "adopted Socialism as its aim"*.

And since then, without wanting to be cynical, the aim of the Labour Party has been to taste the sweet fruits of office. It has supported two world wars — in spite of the fact that among its objectives was that of:

> "co-operating with the Labour and Socialist organisations in other countries and assisting in organising a Federation of Nations for the maintenance of Freedom and Peace . . . "

* *The Labour Party in Perspective* by C.R. Attlee. (Left Book Club, 1937).

In 1929 as the largest Party in the House it took office under Ramsay Macdonald who, according to Mr. Attlee, "seemed to think that by a course of studious moderation he could conciliate opposition, while doing enough to retain the support of his own followers". Then in 1931, Macdonald who had

> for some years been more and more attracted by the social environment of the well-to-do classes, (who) had got more and more out of touch with the rank and file of the Party, while the adulation which is almost inseparable from the necessary publicity given to the leader of a great movement had gone to his head and increased his natural vanity [and] the philosophy of gradualness which he had always maintained became almost indistinguishable from Conservatism.

Macdonald in 1931 "betrayed those who had given him their trust" and formed the National Government. The Labour Party in the House was reduced to a "handful" under the "very able leadership of George Lansbury". In 1937 Mr. Attlee was writing that the Party was "the alternative force in politics to Capitalism", adding:

> More than ever today there stands out the difference between the two systems, Socialism and Capitalism. Liberalism as a coherent philosophy of politics is dead. What was of value in it has been taken over by Labour, and some part of its spirit has even gone towards modifying Conservatism.

The fact that after the elections of 1959 there is talk either of an *entente* between Labour and Liberals or of the replacement of Labour by the Liberals as the second Party, only goes to show that *plus ça change,* etc. . . . or that those who are always taken for a political ride are the mugs, the public!

In view of Mr. Attlee's subsequent acceptance of office in a war-time Coalition Government, his unequivocal opposition to Popular-Fronts in 1937 is interesting as well as revealing. And what of his own achievements when he was leader of a Party with an absolute majority in the House immediately after the war and when radical change was acceptable not only in this country but in a war-exhausted world at large? Did he heed his good advice to Socialists?

> The Labour Party stands for such great changes in the economic and social structure that it cannot function successfully unless it obtains a majority which is prepared to put its principles into practice. Those principles are so far-reaching that they affect every department of the public services and every phase of policy. *The plain fact is that a Socialist Party cannot hope to make a success of administering the Capitalist system because it does not believe in it.* This is the fundamental objection to all the proposals that are put forward for the formation of a Popular Front in this country (Our italics).

In 1959 the Labour Party puts forward a programme which in effect tells the people *that it can operate the Capitalist system more effectively than the Capitalists* (that is, the Tories). The Public, even without Lord Attlee's pre-war Left Book Club best-seller to guide them, intuitively feel that the Tories know more about how to run the capitalist system than the "socialist" dons, and so vote for them — we are now talking of the "don't knows", the "floating voters", not the conservative-Conservatives and the conservative-labourites who will vote Tory or Labour respectively even if an H-bomb explosion blows them onto the moon.

Socialism, as Mr. Attlee pointed out in 1937 has nothing in common with, indeed it is the antithesis of, capitalism. It is the advocacy of co-operation as opposed to cut-throat competition; it is equality not privilege; it is production for use and need and not for profit.

The Labour Party then, according to its Objects, want Socialism, but in practice want power — within the limits of the Constitution, of course. This means, quite simply, winning a majority of votes in the Constituencies.

Since the Tory Party (and now the Liberals) have the same objective and, apart from their control of, or influence on, sections of mass-communications, also depend on votes in order to be returned to "power", it is clear that all parties must concentrate their resources on winning votes rather than in educating the people politically.

To this end the Tories have perforce been obliged to share the cake of economic prosperity more widely and curb the 19th century ambitions of the *ultras* in their ranks, while the Labourites have removed the (false) teeth of their Bevans in the name of unity. So the Tories are a shadow of the free-enterprise buccaneers they once were and the Labourites a poor copy of their original selves, a mere party seeking "to maintain in Parliament and the country a political Labour Party" . . . by hook or by crook! — And the public voted accordingly!

[October 24, 1959]

CALLING ALL SOCIALISTS!

If we again return to the subject of the Labour Party's election post-mortem we hope it will not be inferred that we are either interested in resuscitating the corpse, or of offering advice on how to win the next elections. But we are interested in reaching the socialists among the twelve million people who voted Labour and among the seven million who didn't vote at all. And the best time to try to remove illusions about Socialism-via-the-ballot box is surely now and not at election-time, when though admittedly people are more politically conscious, their objectivity is pitifully taxed by sentimental political loyalties, promises by one of the parties on issues on which they feel strongly, or simply because they would hate the local Tory to win by the one vote they might not cast against him.

If the Labour leaders have got a lot of re-thinking to do between now and the next elections — if they want to win them — equally socialists and anarchists will need to engage in a lot of thought *and action* if in the meantime they want to make some progress along the road towards socialism and the free society.

Mr. Bevan was quite right when he declared that the defeat of the Labour Party did not imply a final rejection of socialism by the British electorate. Had the Labour Party campaigned on an uncompromising socialist programme, it may well have lost more votes than it did. But that was not the problem, declared Mr. Bevan. The programme on which the Labour Party fought the election could only be described as similar to that of "pre-1914 liberalism brought up to date".*

But welcome as Mr. Bevan's declaration is, the fact remains that for a very large section of the public, socialism is represented by the Trade Unions and the Labour Party. So that, what with the policies it advocates and the imaginary policies attributed to it by the gutter press to chill the spines of its gullible, respectable, readers, the present generation's picture of socialism is understandably more like *The Picture of Dorian Gray* than *The Soul of Man Under Socialism.*

It already seems clear that the Labour Party's "re-thinking" will develop along two lines at least. On the one hand the fanatical ballot-boxers for whom winning elections has become an end in itself; on the other those who believe (until the next election?) that the *raison d'être* of the Labour Party is the implementation of

*We quote from his article published in the Paris weekly *l'Expres* (Oct. 16).

socialist policies, according to *their* understanding of socialism, of course.

Re-thinking for the former will not involve re-reading the socialist texts of Blatchford, Morris and Cole. For them what the Labour Party needs are Public Relations men, advertising experts and psychologists (not forgetting "experts" like Mr. Robert McKenzie who was busily carving up the Party in last Sunday's *Observer** so that apparently, it could function better next time). More national advertising and less nationalisation; more Public Relations Officers and less of the Public Ownership nonsense; more socialites in the Party and fewer socialists.

Not only has the prostrate Labour Party been obliged to listen to its garrulous Douglas Jay advocate in print for all to read that it should drop nationalisation and change its name, but the reappraisals of some of the other top intellectuals are far from reassuring. For instance, Mr. R.H.S. Crossman (sacked from his column by the *Daily Mirror* who also have been re-thinking their pro-Labour policy in the light of a falling circulation), writing in the *New Statesman* explains Labour's loss of votes in these terms:

> In this era of Tory prosperity a Labour opposition has to run very fast to stay where it is. Each year which takes us further, not only from the hungry Thirties but from the austere Forties, weakens class consciousness. And if nothing is done to stop this national tendency, more and more Socialist voters turn first into don't knows and then into active Tories. It is my belief that the campaign which Hugh Gaitskell led is the only thing which prevented a catastrophic landslide last Thursday. Without it we might have lost not twenty-three but up to a hundred seats, and been left with virtually no representation south of the Trent. What we achieved was a last minute rally which enabled us to poll our loyal vote throughout the country, and even to make some middle of the roaders consider the possibility of voting Labour.

A Labour Party "running very fast in order to stay where it is" in "this era of Tory prosperity" is a somewhat confusing image, for

*"Labour's Need for Surgery" (*The Observer,* 25/10/59). In this article Mr. McKenzie proposes that anybody in the Labour Party who was troubled by principles should leave the Party and join a "new I.L.P.", in which "there is certainly a place" for those "who in the American phrase 'would rather be right than be President' ". having scoured the Party clean of any principled elements it could then concern itself with the real issues. "Politics will be about how we should share between us the burdens and benefits of the 'mixed economy plus Welfare State' which clearly reflects the basic consensus among us in domestic affairs. The proposals for a capital gains tax is exactly the sort of issue which illuminates the real difference between the parties in domestic affairs". How right he is! But on what social grounds does he suggest that this state of affairs should be perpetuated?

"Tory prosperity" would imply that the stage is moving forward, in which case the Labour Party is running backwards. Why should it bother to run backwards in order to stay where it is? As Bevan put it in his *l'Expres* article, if one has to understand the reason why a majority of the electorate voted Tory and adjust the Party's policy accordingly, then "from a logical point of view it means that we should all join the Conservative Party, since it is manifest that it is the Party closest to the present feelings of the electorate".

The more realistic view is, to our minds, put forward by those who think the Labour Party should move to the Left rather than to the Right — more realistic, let us hasten to add, not because we think they will achieve socialism through the ballot box, but because they will in fact survive as a Party, albeit as an opposition, whereas the Crossman and Jay roads will inevitably lead to the absorption of the Labour Party by the Tories and the Liberals, with the principled socialists, who "would rather be right than be President" either giving up the struggle or, as we hope, seeing that there is something, after all, in what the anarchists have been saying for these past hundred years.

Barbara Castle writing in the same issue of the *New Statesman* concluded that

> Labour's function is to civilise society economically, so that men and women are educated by their environment in a sense of community and in a wider vision of self-interest than the pursuit of a higher and higher individual wage. If we forget this lesson while learning others that must certainly be learnt — lessons of organisation, of presentation, of the need for more political courage — then the Labour Party will die from the inside, and men of conscience and social vision will turn away from us.

What a vindication of the so-called "negative" attitude of the anarchists, coming from the Labour Party's chairman!

At the October 8, General Elections, the Labour Party were hoist with their own petard, and we were neither surprised nor sorry. If anybody wishes to criticise our position on the grounds that by our attitude we reveal an indifference to the fate of the working classes, the Nyasas and the cause of Nuclear Disarmament, our reply is that whatever government is in office the system remains, and it is not by changing governments but by fighting the system that the people will eventually free themselves*.

As to the fate of the Nyasas, if twelve million voters for the Labour party feel sufficiently strongly about the issue of Federation are we to believe that they have neither the wit nor the energy to take action which will convince any government where its interest lies in the matter? (Quite apart from the fact that the issue of Federation will be decided by the Nyasas themselves ultimately, whatever the government decides next year).

Finally, on the question of nuclear disarmament, who among the members of the Labour Party has the impertinence to suggest that a Labour government offers greater prospects of achieving these ends than a Tory administration? It is true that only this week Lord Attlee told an Australian radio audience that he proposed to spend the rest of his life "fighting for world disarmament". Yet only a few months ago, in the *Observer* we read an article of his in which he expressed his approval of President Truman's action in pressing the button which launched the A-bombs that annihilated, maimed or subjected to a slow and painful death, thousands of civilians in Hiroshima and Nagasaki. Nor have we forgotten that it was Bevan who at the Labour Party conference in 1957 refused to support a motion calling on this country to ban the Bomb "unilaterally".

In quoting Barbara Castle as being more "realistic" than the Jays and the Crossmans who, it seems to us, are the liquidators of the Labour Party, we are nevertheless not seduced by her references to a "sense of community" and "wider vision of self-interest". These people want to eat their cake and have it; they want a sense of community and at the same time a government with executive powers; they want something nobler than "self interest linked to a higher and higher individual wage" yet never attack the money system; indeed they fall over backwards to assure the public that their "socialism" encourages the ambitious person to "get on" — within the capitalist system. They talk of the egalitarian system, yet when have they suggested pensioning-off the Monarchy and its horsey retinue? They pose as internationalists by definition, yet this is the kind of tripe served up on *Tribune's* front page after the defeat:

> Under the Tories, Britain is doomed to be a back number among the nations. A certain narrow, blinkered, lazy kind of comfort — the kind with which so many voters have just shown themselves satisfied — may be maintained. But neither economically, socially, nor in the achievement of world stature and leadership can Britain seize the chances that should be ours.

*As Attlee was pointing out in his *The Labour Party in Perspective* (1937) "Such liberty as they (the majority of the people) have got as workers has been the fruit of long and bitter struggles by the Trade unions (p.141) . . . Factory inspectors are necessary because many employers lack social sense . . . Their presence is not due to the Socialist but the anti-Socialist spirit" (p.143).

By a "back number" they mean statistically, output of steel in millions of tons, output of cars, refrigerators, and why not bombers and missiles as well as motorways and nylon panties? Surely for the socialist, as for the anarchist, the influence that a nation can exert on world affairs, and towards internationalism, is its ability to submerge its identity as a nation and to direct its attention and its message not to politicians but to the peoples of the world. What do these demagogues mean by "world stature and leadership"? Socialists should think in terms of co-operation, example, identity with the people in all territories. But how can they even start thinking in those terms without first rejecting centralised authority (government) in our social relations, and the capitalist system (production for profit), in our economic relations?

As Mr. Attlee put it in 1937 when the "responsibilities of office" had not warped his objectivity:

> The abolition of classes is fundamental to the Socialist conception of society. Whatever may be the professions of belief in democracy made by the supporters of the present system, they do, in fact, think it right and natural that there should be class distinctions.

But the Labour Party *believe in the present system.* The trouble, according to the Party's *enfant terrible* "Tribune", is that the Tories don't know how to run the system.

> With a properly planned effort, Britain could advance to the standard of living taken for granted in America and now confidently expected by Russia's young generation. But the Tories have successfully hidden the need for such an effort.

So when we "advance to the standard of living taken for granted in America" we've got Socialism? So there's socialism in America after all, in spite of the fact that big business is in control and the Republicans are in office?

Come off it, *Tribune!* Socialism, surely, is made of sterner stuff!

[October 31, 1959]

VOTES OR SOCIALISM?

One of the most often repeated themes at the Labour Party's week-end conference at Blackpool was that in order to attract the young people of to-day the Party needed a New Look. As Mr. Gaitskell put it:

> We have got to show that we are a modern mid-twentieth-century party, looking to the future and not to the past. We must have, for example, modern-looking party premises situated in the right place. In the main street, newly painted and decorated brightly. Attractive and appealing to the public of 1959. They are not all like that today.

But apart from an attractive shop front to draw them in, Mr. Gaitskell thought they should

> put more stress on the issues which specially appeal to younger people. I believe these include the cause of colonial freedom; the protection of the individual against ham-handed and arrogant bureaucracy; resistance to the squalid commercialism which threatens to despoil our countryside and disfigure our cities; a dislike of bumbledom in all forms; a great concern for sport and the arts.

If this is indeed what the younger people are specially interested in to-day what then is all the pother about?

Mr. Bevan too, winding up the inquest, dealt at length with youth. During the past ten years a great number of young people had had their material conditions improved and their status rose in consequence.

> Temporarily, their personalities are satisfied with the framework in which they live. They are not conscious of discontent or frustration or limitations. What is our lesson? We must enlarge and expand these personalities so that they become conscious of limitations and restrictions. The problem is one of education. This affluent society is an ugly society. It is a society in which the priorities are all wrong. The language of priorities is the religion of socialism.

Fine sentiments into which one can read a call to rebellion against the false values of this "vulgar" society. But what then did he mean when later he declared that "the flower of youth goes abroad because there are no opportunities at home"? The flower of our youth as he called them are the people who go abroad because they can earn more money in Canada, America, Australia, etc. . . than in Britain. Mr. Bevan was surely not suggesting that these societies are any less "vulgar" or "ugly" than the motherland?

Another speaker put the point that by 1964 there would be voters to whom the names of Attlee, Stalin and Churchill will mean little or nothing. Presumably this was an argument in favour of a forward-looking Labour Party and not one living in the past. But while we are not alarmed nor surprised by the prospect of oblivion for the politicians, the more serious prospects are that by 1964 socialism will mean little or nothing to the public!

It is utter nonsense to say that the Labour Party is living in the past. Of no party which has come forward with a pension scheme which will reach full maturity in the year 2004 can it be said either that it is living in the past or that it has not a care for the future of the youth of to-day. An allegedly socialist party which shows such an undying faith in the money system that it can envisage it still flourishing in 2004 has indeed shaken away the cobwebs of a past which envisaged a world freed from capitalism and the coin by which it maintains the class divided, the privilege ridden, society.

How right was the speaker who suggested that it would be advisable for the labour movement to do less talking and more thinking. It is clear that whatever else it lacks, and that includes the Tories' money, modern shop fronts, poster campaigns and such like, the movement has an abundance of soapbox orators who get easily carried away by the fluency of their own tongues. The confusion that ensues can only be gauged by *reading* what was said. We have already cited one example on youth. But the most glaring case of confusion was the use of terms such as "nationalisation", "public ownership", and "common-ownership" by speaker after speaker in which they were used as synonyms or as distinct terms to suit each particular speaker's argument. Even Mrs. Castle, who said some interesting things, confused government and community, State and public. Above all she and the other 3,000 delegates whatever their differences of interpretation, of ends and means, were meeting at Blackpool to hold an inquest on the October defeat and to find the formula for victory next time. And from the viewpoint of achieving socialism this unity was much more of a stumbling block than the divergence of opinion such as it was, which, to our minds, could be considered as the only positive aspect of the conference.

If, as Mrs. Castle maintained, the Labour Party has "spent 50 years of political life proving to the people of this country that economic and social morality go hand in hand" it is clear from the results that they have been singularly unsuccessful. As Mr. Gaitskell pointed out, the Welfare State, and the planning of the economy, even by the free enterprise Tories, which ensured full employment ("Minor recessions we shall have — yes"), were the work of the 1945 Labour

Government. Yet in spite of the fact that Labour's election programme sought to extend what it had started in 1945, the electorate voted Tory. And he concluded: "Unfortunately, gratitude is not a reliable political asset" — a conclusion Churchill drew in 1945 when though proclaimed the architect of victory he was ignominiously thrown out at the elections. Which all goes to "prove" that unthinking sheep are most unreliable and unpredictable when you suddenly appeal to them to be rational or logical. For three weeks in every five years the public is urged to show an interest in political and social problems, to know where its true interest lies as well as that of the community. And where the latter clashes with the former to opt for the common good. For the other four years and forty-nine weeks it's jungle warfare aided and abetted by whatever government is in power.

Socialism — any more than anarchism — hasn't a chance of winning an election. For when socialists will be in a majority the electoral system will have long since been dispensed with. That is surely obvious. Socialism is individual responsibility, is social and political awareness, is class consciousness (yes, but not in the sense of wanting to perpetuate classes, but the consciousness of their existence, an understanding of why they exist, and a determination, informed by knowledge and militancy, to abolish them). Government, however benevolent, is the denial of individual responsibility, the opium of social and political awareness and the perpetuator — and creator, *vide* Russia — of classes and class distinction. The Labour movement (by which we mean the rank and file — the leaders don't interest us) must choose between winning elections and furthering the cause of socialism. As a professional politician Bevan is surprisingly naive if he really believes that the "lesson" to be learned from the reactions of the young voter is that "we must enlarge and expand these personalities so that they become conscious of limitations and restrictions. The problem is one of education". That is the lesson for socialists, but surely not for political office-hunters. You only expand personalities, etc. through education, *at the expense of the voting booths.*

If the Labour movement believes that only in occupying the government benches can it "serve the public interest" then it should cut out any ideological cackle and concentrate on raising vast sums of money and think up more popular gimmicks than the Tories or Liberals in time for the next elections. If on the other hand it believes in socialism, in Mrs. Castle's "economic and social morality", or even in Gaitskell's social and racial equality, social justice, and a classless society*, then only by education and example on the one hand, and by attacking capitalism remorselessly at its weakest points, and by withdrawing power from government by starving it of social initiative, on the other, can socialists at the same time weaken the class society and start building the free, socialist, world of to-morrow.

"We are told" — declared Mrs. Castle — "that we have succeeded so well in reforming capitalism that we have made it, not only civilised but practically indestructible". That summing up gives too much credit to the *influence* of the Labour movement even as a force of reaction, but there is no denying that social democracy throughout the world has acted as the indispensable agent of capitalism if only by its betrayal of the workers. And at Blackpool nothing that was said convinces us that the "re-thinking" in the past two months will induce the Labour movement as constituted to venture along the road of socialism, if only because the leadership has a stake in the "ugly", "vulgar" society of the present.

Only a month before the Election Mr. Gaitskell bought £6,000 worth of shares in a finance outfit called "Invest for Success"; only recently in the Commons "row" over the £4,000 per annum pension to the former Speaker of the House in view of his appointment as Governor General of Australia at £10,000 per annum, Mr. Gaitskell was reported as saying that he did not think the ex-Speaker's pension was excessive. Obviously for Mr. Gaitskell "some are more equal than others". But we do not wish to "pick on" Mr. Gaitskell for, apart from a few honourable exceptions, all the leadership, and sponsors, of the Labour movement are doing very nicely in spite of the "ugliness" and "vulgarity" of existing society. And so long as they live off the fat of the land there is no reason why anyone should listen to them. Mr. Bevan said it was a question of education (in socialism and revolt presumably). The first lesson in that education is *example by the teacher*. And until that is realised Mr. Bevan can go on spouting socialism until his cows come home.

[December 5, 1959]

*These were among Mr. Gaitskell's "basic first principles" as expressed at Blackpool.

SERVE NO MASTER

The appointment of Mr. Alfred Robens, M.P. — a former Minister of Labour in the Attlee government — as industrial relations officer to Atomic Power Construction Ltd. has been roundly condemned by Mr. Ted Hill, the boilermakers' leader, in a report to his members. Bearing in mind Mr. Robens' views, expressed last year, that strikes in the second half of the twentieth century were an anachronism, Mr. Hill declared:

> I do not think strikes are an anachronism in a capitalist society but I do believe that the appointment of Socialist M.P.s as labour advisers to hard-boiled capitalists is an anarchronism and therefore the Labour Party Executive should look into this matter, as Labour M.P.s cannot serve two masters.

When asked to comment on the appointment of Mr. Robens, the Minister of Power in the Tory government leapt to his defence with the following observations

> "When Mr. Robens was Minister of Labour one of his jobs in that capacity was to make industrial relations in this country run as smoothly as possible. That I understand is the purpose of his new job. Therefore I cannot see there would be any more controversy about this job than there was when he was Minister of Labour"

which were logical enough but could hardly be expected to satisfy Mr. Hill unless, of course, one believes that two wrongs make a right. As Mr. Hill pointed out in reply: "the issue was one of serving the trade union and Labour movements, and if this service was incompatible to the individual because he desired to serve an employer he should leave the movement". But in his turn, Mr. Hill has not dealt with the argument of the Minister of Power as unequivocally as he has dealt with Mr. Robens' present action.

In his original comment Mr. Hill said that "Labour M.P.s cannot serve two masters". It is quite clear who one of the masters he had in mind was: "the hard-boiled capitalist". What is not clear to us is the identity of the other "master". The Labour M.P. is sent to Parliament by the votes of a majority of his constituents and is expected to represent the interests and to express the point of view of all his constituents, though in reality he votes according to a policy determined by the Party Executive and enforced by the Party Whip. That same Party at each general election aims at winning sufficient support at the polling booths to entitle it to form its own government. And behind that Party, dominating it financially and numerically are the Trade Unions.

A Labour government, as we know from the experience of 1945-50 when the Labour Party enjoyed an absolute Parliamentary majority, though professing to further the cause, the interests, of the "working classes", of the "under-privileged", was much more concerned with operating the machine of State successfully — which means maintaining its authority and balancing budgets — than with seeking to achieve the ends of socialism. During its years in office the Labour government took no steps to introduce a more human and commonsense approach to production and distribution, did nothing to curb the ambitions of industrialists or the power of money values and the cult of materialism.

Nationalisation was a damp squib the moment it was clear that the workers in those industries had only changed masters, and that profit was the criterion by which they were judged. Even if we accept that the money system could not be abolished overnight, a government which seeks to scrape up a few million pounds from a public levy on doctors' prescriptions, which tries to make public transport "pay its way" by insisting that those who use it should not only pay running costs but generously compensate former shareholders, and at the same time glibly squanders more than a thousand million pounds sterling a year on power politics, euphemistically described as "defence", such a government can hardly be described as safeguarding, and by no stretch of the imagination as *forwarding,* the interests of the working sections of the population.

The question we would put to Mr. Hill is: "Who is the other master?" If we have understood him correctly, it is "the Trade Union and Labour movements", in which case we insist that from the point of view of the workers nothing has changed, and no principle is involved when a Labour Member of Parliament, who was a Minister of Labour in a former Labour government, is appointed as the industrial relations officer to a capitalist enterprise. Neither the Labour Party nor the Trade Unions has any intention of abolishing the capitalists or the system. Perhaps we should remind Mr. Hill of the statement issued by the T.U.C. when the Tories won the elections of 1951:

> It is our long-standing practice to work amicably with whatever government is in power . . . There need be no doubt, therefore, of the attitude towards the new government.

And if the T.U.C. aims at working amicably with all governments what grounds has Mr. Hill to complain when the Labour movement manages to place a fifth-column in the very stronghold of the enemy? Mr. Hill argues, rightly to our minds, that no man can see, and advance, both the workers' point of view and serve (at a salary) the bosses' interests. It is true that an enlightened boss may see the wisdom of employing a man as his industrial relations officer who "understands" the workers' problems, but let no one over-estimate the *enlightenment* of such a boss. His principle concern is to achieve maximum productivity, not happy or satisfied workers. If the latter can be used as a means to the former, which is the ends, why not appear in the guise of the unorthodox, the eccentric, the "progressive" boss? But, say the revisionists, is it not better from the workers' point of view to have such a boss than the old-fashioned, classic, boss who looks on psychology as a new-fangled idea and who thinks that workers should be kept in their place?

We can only answer that question by the realist approach of putting ourselves in Mr. Robens' shoes. There are two kinds of power; the one based on experience, knowledge, the other based on authority. The former expresses itself through discussion, the latter through power. Whatever the origins of Mr. Robens' success story, his advancement first as M.P., then as Minister of Labour (incidentally, his ministerial status was made possible by a reshuffle of the Labour Cabinet, caused by the resignations of Bevan and Wilson, on matters of "principle") indicate a career approving and relying on the principle of government and the power of an elite. Certainly no indication that the values, social and economic, on which the system was based should be opposed or even questioned. And before Mr. Hill condemns Mr. Robens he should ask himself whether the Trade Unions can, on their record, adopt a holier-than-thou attitude towards Labour politicians who seek to cash in in a world which idolises the realist and despises the "idealist".

To our minds there can be no *modus vivendi,* no understanding, between capital and labour. No employee, no human being *in his senses* will ever accept, freely, a situation in which he depends on the whim of a fellow-being for his means of existence. This is the fundamental issue, for no employer, large or small, can create a feeling of security in the mind of his employee (quite apart from creating the feeling that the employer is aware of his worth in money terms).

Even the least socially-conscious worker never looks upon his employer as a philanthropist. Why indeed, should he be? But equally why should the worker be a philanthropist who sells his labour power to an employer whose only interest in him is to profit by his labour? Consciously or unconsciously these attitudes persist, in spite of so-called full employment and record profits, and the "voice of reason" of such now respectable (sometimes unorthodox) organs of the Press as the *Guardian* which suggested that the alternative to the Robens line is industrial strife and unemployment, strikes and lock-outs "and wages rather around 30s. a week" instead of "conciliation" and "full employment".

We are not surprised when the organs of the Press, which see themselves if not as pillars, then, at any rate, as accepted fomenters of thoughtful public opinion, talk a lot of conformist nonsense. But when a minority paper such as the *Socialist Leader* devotes a whole editorial to exposing the duplicity of politicians such as Michael Foot ("Foot in both Camps") without drawing the conclusion that perhaps power politics is *per se* the cause of the very moral dishonesty of which the *Socialist Leader* complains, one feels that after all the anarchist denunciation of politics is not a waste of breath, however much it may appear to some as a voice in the wilderness.

The final paragraph of the *Socialist Leader's* editorial rightly, we think concludes

> Foot (who dislikes intensely the idea of Mr. Gaitskell as leader of the Labour Party) may strike many people as being very sincere; he must also strike them as being very illogical. For, if he really believes all that he says in criticism of Gaitskell and the Labour Party, he couldn't in all honesty plead with people to vote Labour. And, so long as he does, we shall regard him as a man with a foot in both camps.

But whereas the *Socialist Leader* believes that the alternative for workers is between voting for the Labour Party and the Independent Labour Party; for George Stone and not Michael Foot, we anarchists draw the conclusion from all this evidence that the alternative is between voting and not voting, between abdicating what power we have to political parties, and using it individually and collectively for our emancipation.

Mr. Hill objects to Mr. Robens' acceptance of a job as an Industrial Relations Officer on the grounds that he cannot "serve two masters". We, on the other hand, object to any man serving a master at all, which probably explains why we, though sympathetic to Mr. Hill's criticism of Mr. Robens' appointment, are nevertheless critical of the grounds for his objections.

[January 30, 1960]

NOTES FOR THOSE ABOUT TO BE DOUBLE-X ED.

A few more days and the battle of words will be over, the tons of printed matter will be finding their way onto the rubbish dumps and into the pulp mills; the faces of the leaders on a thousand hoardings will be obliterated by "Beer is Best" or "Thinking Men smoke Cigars" or "You've never had it so white" posters; the votes will have been counted, the winning candidates declared; the new government formed. For a few weeks the political analysts, wise after the event, will be trying to show how right their forecasts were, however wide of the mark they may have been, and then the country will sink back into political apathy for another five years. For whichever party wins life for the people of this country will go on much the same as it has been these past five years, and they will have as little real voice in the nation's affairs whichever party takes office. Indeed, for about three months (counting the summer recess) Parliament has not been functioning, and during the past month Cabinet Ministers have been proclaiming their worth from public platforms up and down the country . . . and yet the machine of State works on as smoothly or as inefficiently (according to your party allegiance) as ever.

Whatever differences of objectives divide the two main parties (and we have tried to demonstrate in previous articles that they are differences of emphasis and not of principle) what is clear in the programmes of both parties is that the people will still have no voice in their affairs; that the existing political and economic machine will go on determining our "values" and our "objectives" which thoughtful, radical people this past century have invariably condemned as inhuman, unjust as well as wasteful of human energy and resources.

According to all three parties the panacea for a "New Britain" is contained in the magic "Four per cent." growth in production each year. Yet it is, as a writer put it in last week's *Observer,* not only an "ideological escape hatch for politicians of all parties" but that "growthmanship is the cult of making everybody better off without affecting the structure of society". These words of wisdom were, surprisingly enough, penned by Sir Jock Campbell, head of the huge trading concern, the Booker Group, who, if we understand him correctly, has penetrated the smokescreen of wealth and status to discover that the values of to-day are all wrong, artificial, and do not fulfil the individual.

Now while it is probably true that there are few tycoons thinking along the lines of Sir Jock Campbell, and fewer still who will give up their wealth and power to seek to put into practice their social beliefs, we believe that in the years that lie ahead we shall see the beginnings of a social conscience among the growing number of people who have achieved affluence and status in society only to discover that in so doing they have lost, or are denied, values which money cannot buy, which governments cannot legislate for, however well-intentioned, and without which affluence, prosperity, material success are empty achievements.

The fundamental difference between the parties — declared Lord Attlee in St. Pancras the other day — is that "the Conservatives believe everything must be worked for a profit, and Labour believes in service to the community". If the distinctions were true, then it is difficult to understand why Labour should not win the present contest hands down, or that the Conservatives handsomely won the last three elections, after the post-war landslide to Labour. It is more true to say, as the *Guardian* did, that "only a minority of Labour Party members — and a tiny minority of supporters — want a fully socialist society. And only a small minority of Conservatives want to let the market rip". Or, as Iain MacLeod wrote in the *Sun;* "All the parties and all their candidates long to see peace and prosperity, and any politician who pretends otherwise is a charlatan". Apart from the fact that no politician could ever hope to be elected if he preached war and poverty for the masses, capitalism in this age of technology and automation has adjusted to the idea of widespread consumerism without thereby abandoning the class society which confers power as well as greater prosperity on a privileged minority.

The possibilities are, and certainly this must be what the ruling classes hope for, that we shall in due course find ourselves living as well-fed, well-housed and well-clothed contented cows without a care in the world or a rebellious thought in our heads. We believe instead that the more affluent we become, the more education our children receive, the more leisure we may enjoy with automation, the more dissatisfied will we become with the values of the acquisitive society, and the more stifled by the routine, the dreariness of our daily lives. We, in the affluent West, will also have to take into account the growing frustration of the peoples of the non-affluent world which will manifest itself in different ways, moral as well as military, until an equitable solution of the socio-economic problems on an international scale are arrived at.

We have touched on these questions in order to react against the faint-hearted on the revolutionary Left who see every step in the direction of economic prosperity, at least in the West, as nails in the coffin of revolution and anarchism.

It has some significance when a tycoon explains that he is voting Labour because

> I don't like the present structure of society, however much production grows. In particular I don't like the values and standards it imparts to what used to be called the ruling classes, and through them to the rest of the community. The criteria for these are based largely on aristocratic traditions, and on conventions of behaviour, attitudes and manners . . . They are arrogant values and standards in the literal sense that their upholders arrogate to themselves the assurance that their own standards and values are those of eternity. Whereas in practice they are mostly . . . irrelevant to the real modern world. In this code, moral goodness, aesthetic quality, vision, imagination, cleverness, skill, professionalism, hard work, ambition, score few points. Money, on the other hand, scores a good many.
>
> Thus the present structure of our society brings to the top an unworthy amalgam of aristocratic idealism and plutocratic mediocrity. It seems to me that the High Tories are today's most impractical idealists, trying to live in a bygone aristocratic Utopia.

Sir Jock Campbell is no anarchist revolutionary, and we do not expect him, or Lord Sainsbury or any other pro-Labour Party successful capitalists, to pave the way to a non-capitalist, free society. But that among the tycoons of capitalism are some who are prepared publicly to express a moral uneasiness and a social conscience indicates, so far as we are concerned, that there are moral and social pressures from below day in day out gnawing away at the existing structure of society in spite of a surface skin of apathy, resignation, and successful brainwashing.

Anarchists cannot be uninterested in the coming election results whatever their views about the demerits of the contending Parties. The fact that the anarchist movement has campaigned to persuade people not to use their vote is proof of our commitment and interest. If there is, say, a 60 per cent. poll we will not assume that the 40 per cent. abstentions are anarchists, but we would surely be justified in drawing the conclusion that among that 40 per cent. there are a sizeable minority who have lost faith in political parties and were looking for other instruments, other values. If the Tories are returned to office we cannot ignore the fact that a majority of electors have cast their votes for the traditional party of privilege, just as a similar result in favour of Labour is a vote for the traditional party of the underprivileged, even though we believe that there is nothing, or very little, to choose between a Tory, Labour or Liberal government.

If the anarchists could persuade half the electorate to abstain from voting this would, from an electoral point of view, contribute to the victory of the Right. But it would be a hollow victory, for what government could rule when half the electorate by not voting had expressed its lack of confidence in all governments? In other words, whichever government was in office would be subjected to real pressures from people who believed in their own power. Anarchists call on people not to use their vote and be instead conscious of their power as individuals which, linked to that of others of like mind, can command the respect of governments, can curb the power of governments as millions of crosses on ballot papers never will.

In Britain we have universal suffrage yet a minority rules the country and controls the nation's wealth; women have won the vote but they still live in a man's world; the right of workers to organise is now recognised (and even encouraged) by governments and employers, yet they have failed to win their freedom from wage slavery.

How many of you will think on these grim truths the next time you are exhorted by the politicians to be "responsible citizens" and use your vote?

[October 10, 1964]

About FREEDOM PRESS

Since 1886 FREEDOM PRESS has been concerned with making, as well as encouraging others to make, anarchist propaganda.
Our journals have dealt with the problems of the day as well as keeping readers informed of the activities of the international movement. *Freedom* (monthly, 1886-1927), *Freedom Bulletin* (occasional, 1928-1932), *Spain and the World* (fortnightly, 1936-39), *War Commentary* (monthly/fortnightly, 1939-44), *Freedom* (fortnightly/weekly, 1945— continuing), *Anarchy* (monthly, 1961-70). All this material will shortly be available on microfilm.

FREEDOM PRESS books and pamphlets have dealt both with practical and theoretical questions of concern to anarchists and libertarian socialists. Not only did FREEDOM PRESS publish the first translations of many of the writings of Kropotkin and Malatesta but at a time when the commercial publishers saw no profit in Berkman, Bakunin or Proudhon, nor in Kronstadt, the Spanish collectives or indeed in anarchism FREEDOM PRESS went on publishing. In the late 1940s and early 'fifties we published Alex Comfort's *Barbarism and Sexual Freedom* and *Delinquency,* John Hewetson's *Sexual Freedom for the Young* and *Ill-Health, Poverty and the State,* and in the middle of the last 'war against fascism' FREEDOM PRESS issued John Olday's *March to Death,* a volume of telling anti-war cartoons, and Marie Louise Berneri's *Workers in Stalin's Russia* at a time when all parties from Tories to Trotskyists were united in closing their eyes and ears to the excesses of Stalinism.

Some of FREEDOM PRESS'S current titles will be found overleaf.

FREEDOM PRESS also run a well-stocked bookshop and an efficient mail order service to all parts of the world. Write to us for more details and for a specimen copy of our 16-page journal *Freedom* at **FREEDOM PRESS in Angel Alley, 84B Whitechapel High Street, London E.1**

Badly Drawn Beth

ORCHARD BOOKS
Carmelite House
50 Victoria Embankment
London EC4Y 0DZ

First published in 2016 by Orchard Books

ISBN 978 1 40833 778 3

A CIP catalogue record for this book is available from the British Library.

2 4 6 8 10 9 7 5 3 1

Printed in Great Britain

The paper and board used in this book are made from wood from responsible sources

Orchard Books is an imprint of Hachette Children's Group and published by the Watts Publishing Group Limited, an Hachette UK company.

www.hachette.co.uk

By Knife & Packer

So, I'm being chased through the park by a pack of angry zombies, I've got cake all over my face AND MY MOST **EMBARRASSING** PHOTO EVER IS ABOUT TO APPEAR IN THE SCHOOL MAGAZINE!!!

How did I get here? Let's go back to the beginning ...

It's the weekend and today couldn't be going much better.

What do you get if you mix strawberry milkshakes, my best friend Cordy and a whole afternoon together?

No, not a sticky mess, you get ...

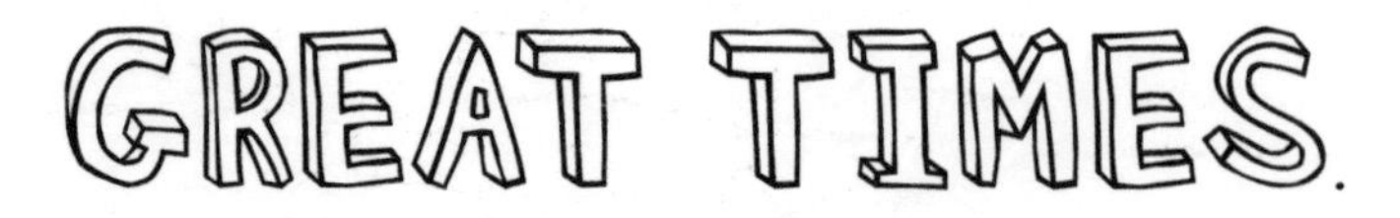

And things are about to get EVEN better ...

"Just you wait until you hear what I've got planned," says Cordy as she takes an ultra loud slurp on her milkshake.

I'm SO excited I almost drop my extra large chocolate chip cookie (it's almost as big as a bin lid) in my milkshake.

"You're going to build that submarine out of old cereal boxes and live in a TROPICAL PARADISE?" I suggest.

"That's next year," Cordy chuckles as she leans in, looks around to make sure no one is listening, and tells me her plan.

"A birthday party!" she whispers.

"No way!" I splutter as milkshake comes out of my nose. "This is great news! We must make it the

ALERT!
WE CANNOT SHOW THIS UNPLEASANT SCENE OF MILKSHAKE COMING OUT OF NOSTRILS!

"That's the only problem," says Cordy. "I'm not sure where to have it, or what sort of cake I should get. Should I have a theme?"

"Just leave it to me," I say, suddenly sounding weirdly confident. "I'll make sure you have the best birthday ever – in fact it will be your very own **BETHDAY!**"

"That would be great," says Cordy. "Are you sure?"

"Of course," I say as my head begins to whir with birthday ideas.

Today is going so well. I am finally enjoying QUALITY TIME. And in my life 'quality time' is about as rare as a pigeon who can ride a unicycle and play the banjo.

Because whenever I'm having a good time, one of the following usually turns up:

BETH'S GUIDE TO QUALITY-TIME WRECKERS

1. My mum and dad. They often appear at embarrassing times and nearly always wearing embarrassing clothes.

OR

2. My sister, Mabel. She usually appears with her uber-annoying study-buddy boyfriend Richard.

3. Mrs Homework.

Mrs Homework is

ALWAYS in a grump.

OR

4. Worst of all, **my arch nemesis Clarissa** – always loud, smug and generally obnoxious.

Today Cordy and I are at the café in the shopping centre while my parents are in the shops. They have **PROMISED** to leave us alone.

"Well, we've got to start with your birthday theme," I begin. "Let's come up with some ideas together."

We **love** coming up with themes, and we immediately start thinking ...

"OK, so obviously it's got to be amazing ..." I muse, as I get my thinking cap on. (Although caps don't really suit me, so instead I put my thinking beret on ...)

First up we **RULE OUT** themes that are not going to work:

1. Fairies – Clarissa's last party was fairy-themed and her dad built her a three-storey FAIRY PALACE in her back garden. We can't beat that and, besides, fairies are not very Cordy.

2. Sport – Izzy, our super sporty friend, recently had a sports party at the local sports centre – he ended up winning **EVERYTHING.**

3. Art – Anju's last party was a pottery and plate painting party – her plates could have been in a museum, our plates could (and actually were) put in the bin.

4. Swimming – Desiree had her party at the local pool and Cordy concluded her hair was allergic to chlorine (and that a sea serpent probably lives at the bottom of the deep end).

I'm just about to suggest some themes that *could* work when I am interrupted by a loud noise.

"Home time!" booms my mum in a voice so loud that it could startle a monkey ... in the middle of a rainforest ... on the other side of the world!

"Beth! Cordy!" blares my dad. "Why are you hiding at the very back of the café?"

We have been happily chatting in the corner but for some reason my parents think they have to be **EXTRA LOUD**. Even though we can hear them perfectly well they seem to SHOUT everything.

Luckily my dad is in a hurry so we are spared seeing his shopping (he did mention something about a new camera device – taking pictures is his latest hobby).

So thinking up the perfect theme for Cordy's party will have to wait ...

It's Monday morning and when Cordy and I arrive at school (we always walk in together) it is great to be able to catch up with all our friends.

Zachary has a new coat.

Sophie has had a haircut.

Then Izzy appears, bouncing a football on his head.

"Hey guys, I had a super-sporty weekend, I went to football camp – it was **awesome**..." he huffs, slightly out of breath from trying to talk and keep a football in the air.

"And I recreated the **Eiffel Tower** in papier mâché!" says Anju, who is good at art.

Finally Clarissa appears and she has her biggest **GLOATING** smile on ... she is wearing **LOTS** of new clothes, and has a shiny new **BAG** – only the smile is the same old smug smile ...

"AND I WENT SHOPPING! BIG TIME! YAY!"

"Woop, woop," mutters Cordy under her breath.

"I wonder where Ms Hailey is?" says Cordy as the school bell rings.

Ms Hailey is our head teacher. She is usually all over the playground, wearing something like a sombrero, high-fiving parents and generally being quite loud.

"She must be plotting something," I say.

"Yes, she's probably in a **haunted house** discussing how her army of ghouls will take over the school," says Cordy, who, like me, has a very 'lively' imagination.

As we take our seats our form teacher, Miss Primula*, uses her slightly scary voice to get our attention.

* pronounced P*RIM*-U-*LA*

"LISTEN UP, CLASS," she barks, after she has taken the register. "It's time to tell you about our brand-new class topic ..."

Although she is small and very nice Miss Primula has a voice that could be used to frighten the barnacles off the bottom of ships ...

"We will be looking at early childhood, babies and toddlers," she announces. "Culminating in a class visit to the Museum of Infancy ..."

This is **GREAT** news – school trips are always fun! Plus, I love museums – even if they haven't yet invented my perfect museum ...

Unfortunately, as I imagine tucking into an exhibit at the Pancake Museum, Miss Primula startles me from my daydream.

"Beth, hello?" she snaps. "Are you awake?"

"Yes, Miss Primula," I mumble, feeling my face go red.

"Great, well, why don't you tell us about your earliest childhood memory," says Miss Primula.

I have to really rack my brain. But then I start to panic and blurt out:

"I remember a trip to a park where I slid down the back of a huge, er, dragon, then, er ... I was chased by a giant pigeon and then it started raining er, chocolate sauce ..."

"Vivid imagination as usual, Beth," Miss Primula says.

A few days later and I am thinking about Cordy's birthday party. This is a **BIG** responsibility and I want to make sure she has the best day ever.

I am discussing this with Scribbles.

He is my pet mouse and I'm sure if he could talk he would have some really refreshing views on subjects like birthday parties and dealing with annoying dads ...

It's then that I notice he is nuzzling my note pad.

"Of course!" I cry. "What I need is a guide to parties!"

In no time I have grabbed a pen and got to work ...

BETH'S GUIDE TO PARTIES

PART 1: PARTY NIGHTMARE ...

THINGS TO AVOID

Parties should be **FUN** but to make sure they are **SUPER FUN,** avoid the following:

Parents: they are great at organising games and laying on the food, but they need to know when to stop being involved.

Sometimes my parents think they are guests and the next thing you know they are joining in the games ...

Food: yes, we like healthy eating but DON'T put sprouts in the cupcakes or broccoli in the biscuits ...

Clothes:

smart is good but DON'T make guests dress up in pink frilly outfits.

BETH'S GUIDE TO PARTIES

PART 2: DREAM PARTY ...

imagine the best party ever!

DO have all your best friends there ... In my dream party I would need a stadium to get all my friends in because I'd be really popular.

Have someone you don't like waiting on you – here's Clarissa with a tray of juices and Richard and Mabel washing up the party plates.

Keep up, Scribbles!

Have a **spotlight** following you around – it is your party after all!

You will need **A LARGE** vehicle for carrying away all your presents ...

A VEHICLE SO BIG IT'S DRIVEN BY A GIANT!

I'm jolted out of my party imaginings by a knock on my bedroom door. When I open it I am greeted by a TINY CLOWN.

"Hello, Beth!" says the mini clown. Now clowns can sometimes be a bit creepy, but this is by **FAR** the creepiest clown I have ever seen.

For once this is NOT the product of my strange imagination. This is real, in fact it's my little brother Bertie. Behind him is my mum.

"So, what do you think?" she asks me. "I did all the make-up myself!"

My mum has been practising STAGE MAKE-UP. After the success of my school talent show, which she organised, she is now working on a play at her new school and has decided to do the make-up herself.

It's all in Badly Drawn Beth Book 2.

You need to read it if you haven't already!

"But I'm not doing very well," says my mum. "My scary characters all look hilarious, and the funny characters all look slightly alarming."

I glance at Bertie and shudder. I see what she means. I try to sound positive.

"I think it needs some work," I say.

"I **overdid** the cheeks, didn't I?" says my mum. "And the lips, they're all wrong ..."

Bertie's fake red nose falls off and his smeary top lip starts to quiver.

I need to say something reassuring. "But with a few tweaks Bertie will make a GREAT clown!" I say. This perks up my baby brother.

I try to explain that I am working on some very important Cordy birthday party ideas and they eventually leave.

In our classroom the next day, Clarissa is doing what she does best. Being all Clarissary (I think I may have invented that word. Feel free to use it if you know someone like Clarissa). She holds up something so bright it hurts my eyes.

"I can't wait for school today," she says in a loud voice. "I have bought a brand-new shiny pencil case – it cost more than most of your family cars!"

Thankfully Miss Primula interrupts her.

"Put that ridiculous thing away, Clarissa, it's so bright it's giving us all a sore head."

I don't think I have ever been happier to start the maths lesson.

Now, I **do** quite like maths but there is always a point when my head starts to get a bit **too** full of numbers.

At this point I wish I had a new best friend – meet **Mr Calculator**.

"Hi Beth, I am your giant walking, talking, calculating friend," Mr Calculator would say. Then I'd introduce him to my sums.

"Pleased to meet you, tricky numbers," Mr Calculator would say. "It would be my pleasure to sort you out ..."

I'm just thinking about how much fun it would be to take Mr Calculator home to meet my annoying older sister Mabel when Miss Primula tells us that the maths lesson is over.

"Now, as you know, this term's theme is early childhood so we will be doing something special in the classroom," she says.

"Woop, woop. What can that be?" whispers Cordy. "Cooking baby food? Setting up a tricycle course?"

"Neither of those, Cordy," grimaces Miss Primula. "And, yes, I really do have amazing hearing. No, we will be installing A Memory Tree ..."

Miss Primula now unveils a cardboard cut-out of a tree. There are already a couple of items attached to it.

"I want everyone to bring in a photo from when you were really young, before you went to school, which we can pin on the tree.

"As you can see, here is a photo of me on my first scooter."

The class ERUPTS with laughter.

"Thank you, yes, calm down, I understand it is quite amusing. Now some of you may be more embarrassed of old photos than others. But I need EVERYONE to bring in a picture," continues Miss Primula.

"So, no picture, no school trip!"

This last line certainly got my attention. I'd better find a picture to bring in. My granny has LOTS of pictures of me as a baby, I'm sure she can help me find one. In fact, I need to speak to her about a cake for Cordy's birthday, so I will have to go there really soon anyway.

We need a theme for Cordy's birthday so she has come over to mine to discuss it. But after a really long day at school if there are TWO things we don't need it's:

1. My annoying older sister MABEL, who still hangs out with her study-buddy/boyfriend Richard

2. My DAD, who has his new HOBBY (thankfully he is taking some time off from his love of karaoke).

We avoid the kitchen to get away from Richard and Mabel but then run straight into my dad in the garden. His new hobby is photography and he recently bought a new camera **AND** a selfie stick. For some reason this means he **POPS UP** everywhere, snapping this and snapping that ... but mostly snapping himself.

Scribbles found him **PRACTICALLY INSIDE** his cage.

We were at the cinema and he was taking pictures of the **POPCORN.**

And Mum had to throw him out of the washing basket **three times** in an afternoon!

"So what's with the camera?" says Cordy.

This is a DISASTER.

"Don't encourage him," I hiss. But it's too late and Dad is now in full **STORYTELLING** mode.

"Thanks for asking, Cordy," says my dad as he settles in to tell us a long story. I won't bore you with the details **BUT** this love of cameras all goes back to his time as a **MALE MODEL** ...

Oh yes, my dad used to work as a model. His favourite look seemed to be **'CHEESY'** and he seemed to mostly pose in chunky knit cardigans ... here are some super-cringeworthy pics from the archive.

Picture 1: Here he is in a speedboat, wearing a **WATERPROOF** cardigan.

Picture 2: Here he is playing golf, wearing a **WINDPROOF** cardigan.

Picture 3: And here he is driving an open-topped sports car, wearing a super light-weight **SUNPROOF** cardigan.

"So you know what I thought?" asks Dad.

But Cordy and I lost track of his story ages ago.

"... so I thought, you know what, I'll buy myself a camera and I will take the pictures, and I will be in most of them! I will then have an exhibition of pictures, all of ME, 'CARDIGAN MAN'" he finishes with a flourish. "Now can I get you guys to pose with ME? That would be GREAT..."

Enough is enough and we decide to say goodbye to Cardigan Man and **GO TO CORDY'S HOUSE**.

NO MABEL AND RICHARD. NO DAD. NO CARDIGANS.

We are now at Cordy's and we are **FINALLY HANGING OUT.**

I should warn you that Cordy's room is all a bit dark and spooky, a bit like her. So there are the outlines of bats on the wall, full-size cardboard cut-outs of werewolves (mostly from the Dusk Light series) and cobwebs over her bed (I'm not sure if these are real or spray-on).

"I have made a list," says Cordy. "It's written in human blood on cursed Ancient Egyptian papyrus."

For a second I imagine Cordy in ancient Egypt, writing her list ...

"Nice new red pen," I say as I look at the list, which is written in red ink in Cordy's spidery handwriting (as you can see, Cordy has a habit of exaggerating things).

1 Theme for my birthday

2 Theme for my birthday

3 Pictures for Memory Tree

4 Talk about Dusk Light

5 Theme for my birthday

6 Theme for my birthday

7 THEME FOR MY BIRTHDAY

"So, from this list I guess our most important task is finding a picture for the Memory Tree," I suggest.

Cordy is about to throw a pillow (shaped like a skull) at me when there's a knock at her door and her mum comes in.

"I've got you strawberry milkshakes," says her mum. "Oh, and I found some lovely old pictures of you as a baby, Cordy ..."

This is EXCELLENT. I love old pictures of people as babies, especially when it's not me.

Cordy squeals.

But Cordy's pictures are not embarrassing at all. In fact, like her, they are super-cool!

"Cordy always was quite, um, unique," says her mum as she opens the photo album. "Look, here she is cuddling a wolf cub at the zoo ...

"And in this one she is eating a lollipop on a visit to a DUNGEON ...

"And here she is feeding some piranhas at the pet shop!"

But by this time Cordy is ushering her out of the room.

"Well, that's your photo sorted," I say. "Now, seriously, we need a theme for your birthday."

We now play theme tennis as we bat ideas backwards and forwards ...

"Pirates," I start.

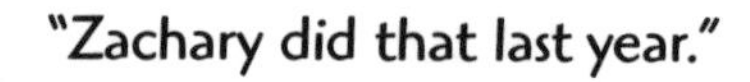

"Too young. What about SUPERHEROES?"

"Zachary did that last year."

We are starting to get desperate!

"GOBLINS?"

"Too scary ..."

"Monkeys?"

"Too hairy."

"OGRES?"

"Too ogre-y."

"Creepy Crawlies?"

"Too crawly, not to mention creepy ..."

This goes on and on and on and on

and we are just about to give up.

It's then I notice Cordy has the latest Dusk Light book.

"Wait a second, what's the latest Dusk Light book all about?" I say, hoping for some inspiration.

Now, as you probably already know, Cordy and I are MAD about Dusk Light. Here is a quick reminder of what it's about ...

In a small American town live a load of cool teenagers.

Even COOLER is the fact that they are actually werewolves ...
1.
2.
3.
4.
They have amazing adventures and I have read all the books and seen all the movies ... and the biggest star is Bobby Gothick.

"It's all about zombies," says Cordy. "The Bobby Gothick character opens up an ancient tomb and zombies appear! It's great ..."

"Great? It's brilliant!" I exclaim. "I think we may have found our theme – ZOMBIES!"

"I love it!" yelps Cordy. "Everyone can dress up. We can have gruesome zombie games and grisly food!"

"And, best of all, NO ONE we know has had a zombie-themed party before," I say, before adding, "... at least, not that I was invited to ..."

"I LOVE IT!" says Cordy.

Now that we have a theme, I can get Granny to make the cake. I call her and arrange to go there on Saturday.

I spend the whole week counting down the days to the weekend.

Finally it arrives and I can visit Granny and talk about making the best cake ever.

"Let's go!" says my dad, who is driving me there. "And don't forget I want lots of pictures with me wearing cardigans: at Granny's, with Otto, under the ..."

I'm no longer listening. Instead I am thinking about Granny and her cakes.

In case you didn't already know, Granny's cakes are A-MA-ZING. Not only do they use HUGE quantities of the scrummiest ingredients ... (no broccoli or cabbage allowed). But she can also make them into the most amazing shapes ...

Recently she baked a SUPER-REALISTIC sponge cardigan for my dad's birthday ...

Then there was an EIGHT TIER chocolate stage for when Mum got her latest job ...

So we can't wait to see what she has got planned for Cordy's birthday cake ...

"Hello! Come right through to the kitchen," says Granny as we walk along the hall. Otto, Granny's parrot, starts pecking at my dad's camera as he tries to take yet another selfie.

Granny's kitchen is an amazing place. As well as endless bubbling pots and incredible smells, there are huge jars filled with chocolate chunks, jelly beans and nuts.

There are also jars, jars and more jars. Jars with raisins in, jars with chocolate buttons and one particularly large jar – the jam jar.

Once I saw a **JAM MONSTER** emerging from the jam jar. For ages I thought it haunted the kitchen at night ... (I later discovered it was my baby brother, Bertie. He had been helping Granny make a cake and he'd fallen face first into the strawberry jam.)

"I have drawn up a plan for Cordy's ZOMBIE cake," says Granny proudly as she shows us a picture. "It's the tallest cake I've ever attempted ..."

It looks incredible! And when Granny describes it, it sounds delicious, too. Well, to me anyway!

"So, it will be GREEN SPONGE, there will be strawberry jam dribbling down it to look like BLOOD and the brain will be almond cake with shocking pink icing ... what do you think?"

"I love it!"

I say, giving Granny a huge hug.

"It doesn't sound that nice to me ..." mutters Dad as he wrestles his camera from Otto.

I'm so excited that I almost forget to ask about photos of me as a toddler.

"Oh, of course my dear, I'll look some out for next time," says Granny as we leave. That means another trip to Granny's – brilliant!

A few days later and Cordy and I are walking to school. Although we are having a PRIVATE CONVERSATION about her birthday cake, a voice suddenly joins in. A voice I don't like hearing first thing in the morning.

Yes, it's number 4 on my list of QUALITY-TIME WRECKERS ... CLARISSA!

"Hey, it's Team Loser!" chuckles Clarissa. "Of course MY birthday cake was made by THIRTY pastry chefs and needed a CRANE to deliver it ..."

She then lets off her Clarissa laugh, which sounds a bit like a horse being tickled. It is NOT a nice noise.

It's at moments like this that I wish the school janitor, Reginald Mavers, would appear with a super-sized GIANT broom and sweep Clarissa out with the rubbish.

But today there is no sign of anyone with a giant broom and Clarissa is being **EVEN MORE ANNOYING** than usual ...

"I can't tell you too much," she gloats, "but there will be some **EXCITING** news today ..."

Clarissa is particularly unbearable when she knows something we don't.

"I know something you don't," she carries on, so excited by this she can hardly stop herself from climbing to the top of the school and shouting it. "It's something to do with Ms Hailey making a BIG announcement ..."

Now, of course, what Clarissa wants is for Cordy and me to beg her to tell us. But we are not going to give her the satisfaction.

"Hey, like we're interested," I say.

"Woop, woop," mutters Cody. We now have our most 'we're not interested' faces on.

'We're not interested' faces are quite useful so here is my guide to using them:

BETH'S GUIDE TO USING YOUR **'I'M NOT INTERESTED'** FACE

1. When your big, swotty sister laughs at your maths homework

2. When your mum tells you that you need to wear smarter clothes to a party

AND

3. When the teacher asks "Why aren't you wearing the regulation school trainers for your P.E. lesson today, Beth?"

The only trouble with my 'I'm not interested' face is that it's really hard to hold for any length of time and we haven't even filed into class when we crack.

"So what is it, what is it, what is it?" I beg. "Just give us an itty, bitty clue ..."

"C'mon, you've got to tell us," says Cordy on her knees. "We'll do ANYTHING, just tell us ..."

"You'll find out soon enough," gloats Clarissa. She is seriously LOVING THIS.

Fortunately, Miss Primula saves us from any more embarrassment.

"Everyone in your places!" she says and we are quickly sitting down. "Now, Ms Hailey will be joining us shortly to tell us about some exciting new developments."

"And I know ALL about them," says Clarissa.

We're in the middle of spelling when there's a knock at the door and Ms Hailey bounces in.

Yes, it's our head teacher, who is quite loud and loves to dress up. But today she is not dressed as a root vegetable (as she was for Healthy Food Week) or dressed as a queen

(as she was for a recent theatre trip).

"Hello, everyone," she says as we wait for the big news.

"From now on there is going to be a brand-new look to SCHOOL CLUBS," announces Ms Hailey. "I've had a bit of a BIG THINK and polished them up, cancelled the ones that aren't working and even brought back some old ones ..."

If we weren't in class Cordy and I would probably jump out of our seats, high-five and start singing in high-pitched voices because this is GREAT NEWS!

As long as I've been at the school the clubs have all been a total disaster ...

There was singing club, when the new singing teacher lost her voice and we sat in silence for most of the sessions.

Astronomy club, when the 'space expert' forgot to take the lens cap off the telescope.

And probably the **most disastrous** of all ...

Science Club, when a 'super safe and fun' experiment involving washing-up liquid and a piece of fudge backfired (literally) and blew off the back wall of the science lab.

"From now on, the school clubs will all be fresh and new and exciting," she proudly announces as she hands out club forms for everyone to fill in.

But before she goes Ms Hailey has a final bit of information for us.

"I would also like to announce one club in particular. A revival of an old club ..."

"Because we are re-launching the school magazine!" blurts out Clarissa.

"Thank you, Clarissa," says Ms Hailey. "Yes, that's right and we are all terribly excited."

This information nearly blows my hair off (if that was possible)!

As she says this I can't help catching Clarissa's eye.

"And I knew it all along ..." she gloats.

So THAT'S what she knew, but how?

I quickly put Clarissa out of my mind, because this is STILL great news. The magazine sounds SO my kind of thing (and Cordy's) that I can hardly sit still.

In fact, I'm so excited I find myself blurting out:

"WE HAVE TO JOIN!"

"Great enthusiasm, Beth," says Miss Primula. "But we need to let Ms Hailey continue."

"Now our school USED to have a magazine," continues Ms Hailey, "It was years ago, back in the days when everything was in black and white. Miss Primula, please."

Miss Primula holds up a dusty copy of the old school magazine. Her face looks like she is holding up something with an unpleasant smell.

"Please pin that up somewhere," continues Ms Hailey.

The greying magazine is now up on the wall at the front of the class.

"Now, this is how **NOT** to do it," she continues, pointing at the faded magazine. "We want the new magazine to be full of great school stories and ..."

Cordy and I, who are sat near the front, can read the headlines. When I really narrow my eyes I can just about read the stories.

"It looks **terrible**," I whisper. "And look how young everyone looks."

"Really, **really** terrible," winces Cordy.

1. JANITOR BUYS NEW MOP

Reginald Mavers bought a new mop recently. He described the mop as "better than my last mop ..." Full story, page 23–27

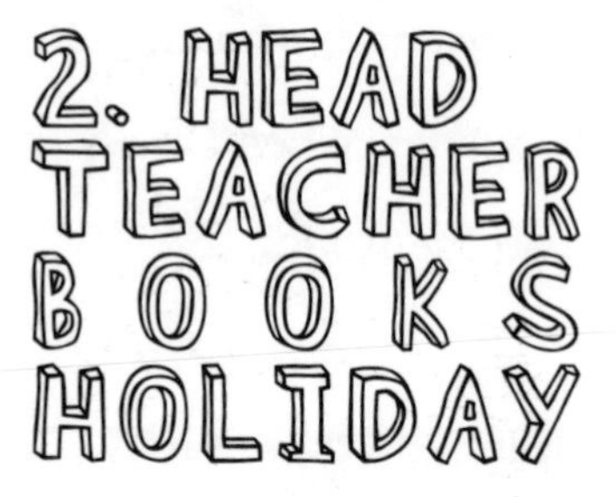

2. HEAD TEACHER BOOKS HOLIDAY

Mr Thompson has booked a long weekend near some old ruins. "I like old ruins and need a break ..." said the popular head teacher. Photos and full story, pages 12–22

3. NEW PASTA SAUCE ADDED TO SCHOOL DINNER MENU

A brand new pasta sauce has been added to the school menu. "It has tomatoes in it ..." said a dinner lady. Recipe and full story, pages 33–45

---

4. SCHOOL ATTENDANCE RECORD SET

A pupil has set a new record for consecutive days without being absent. "I just don't get ill very often ..." said Freddie, aged 8. Full interview on pages 67–88

"Wake up!" I hiss at Cordy, who is startled by my voice. She has fallen asleep at her desk and is starting to snore!

"That magazine is sooo boring," she says, stifling a huge super-sized yawn.

"The new school magazine will be completely fresh and modern," says Ms Hailey. "As well as exciting news from school, we will be looking for some exciting, imaginative stories too!"

Just then there is a knock at the door.

"Oh yes, and we are going to be using the most advanced state-of-the-art printing facilities ever," continues Ms Hailey, as another visitor enters the classroom. "Class, say a big GOOD MORNING to Mr Musgrove."

It's Clarissa's father!

"He runs his own stationery business and has kindly offered to set up all the equipment we need right here in the school to produce the most amazing school magazine ever!" she continues.

Clarissa catches my eye. She is LOVING THIS. **THAT'S** how she knew!

I should probably also mention that MY DAD works for Mr Musgrove's company ... which is, at best, STRANGE and, at worst, really, unnecessarily WEIRD.

Mr Musgrove now starts to talk to us about modern printing methods, lasers, software and lots of other stuff that I don't think anyone understands. In fact, looking around the class I get the impression that ...

Ms Hailey is planning her next wacky outfit ...

Miss Primula is wondering what she will have for lunch ...

And only Clarissa is absolutely starry-eyed and deeply engrossed ...

Thankfully, he eventually finishes and we can get back to maths.

Even though it's a bit off-putting having Mr Musgrove involved, it's not enough to stop me and Cordy from wanting to join and we are the first two to sign up to School Magazine Club*.

*No prizes for guessing who was third ...

When I get home I am so excited about the school magazine I can't wait to tell everyone about it. But I am having one of those afternoons when everyone is too busy to talk ...

My dad is still at work – at least that means he won't suddenly appear as Cardigan Man with his camera ...

My mum is in the study with the door shut – that means something important is going on in there and it's best to avoid disturbing her ...

And Mabel and Richard, who are revising for something like prehistoric medicine, just scoff at me ...

"A printed magazine? That's just so old fashioned ... but you could put a Badly Drawn picture of yourself in there ...*"

*Mabel gave me the nickname Badly Drawn Beth after she spotted some cartoons I did of myself in a PRIVATE notepad. They were not my best work.

I end up going to my room to start thinking up some school magazine article ideas. This is a lot of fun ...

I know the kind of stories that I WOULDN'T like to work on:

No in-depth look at classroom maintenance.

And definitely no interviews with dinner ladies.

And I know the kind of stories I would like to work on ...

QUIRKY AND FUNNY STORIES

These would be interviews with COOL film stars ...

And lots of cartoons and stories and imaginative stuff ...

With my ideas all written down, I now start to think about Cordy's party. But I am rudely interrupted by a **LOUD NOISE**. From experience, I know that these kinds of noises are not generally a good thing.

They are usually a member of my family **DROPPING SOMETHING**, **SPILLING SOMETHING** or **BREAKING SOMETHING**.

Even Scribbles rolls his eyes. (Wiggle the book around for full effect.)

I go downstairs to see what's happened and discover that my DAD looks like he has been attacked by something big and hairy (it looks like he has fur on his face and a strawberry smeared on his lips).

"This has gone too far," my dad says to my mum. "You need professional help ..."

This sounds worrying until I discover my mum has been practising her make-up (again) and was trying to make my dad look like a gorilla (and has actually done a worse job than on Bertie!)

"I promise I'll sign up for a proper theatrical make-up course in the morning," says Mum.

As my dad starts to head off to the bathroom to wash the make-up off I can't resist taking a quick picture of him with his camera! Cardigan Man joins the circus!

Fortunately, the weekend arrives and Cordy and I can concentrate on really important things ... like her birthday. I promised to make it **the best birthday ever** and today we have **two really important jobs.**

So we are in the park, which is where I think the party should be.

"I believe the park is a great choice," I say as we walk towards the barbecue area. "There's lots of space, we can set up games ..."

"The only disadvantage is that the park is right next to school," says Cordy. "I'm not sure I want to be reminded of school on my birthday."

"I know what you mean." I nod. "But as long as there is plenty happening at your party, school will be the last thing on people's minds."

"Mmm, I agree, great idea," says Cordy as she warms to the idea.

Phew, that went well – Cordy likes the venue ...

We now need to talk about **THE GUEST LIST.**

"Soooo," I say. "Who would you like to invite? I have made a list, but you get the final say ..."

I now show Cordy the list I have started working on. I have tried to make it simple but it is actually quite complicated.

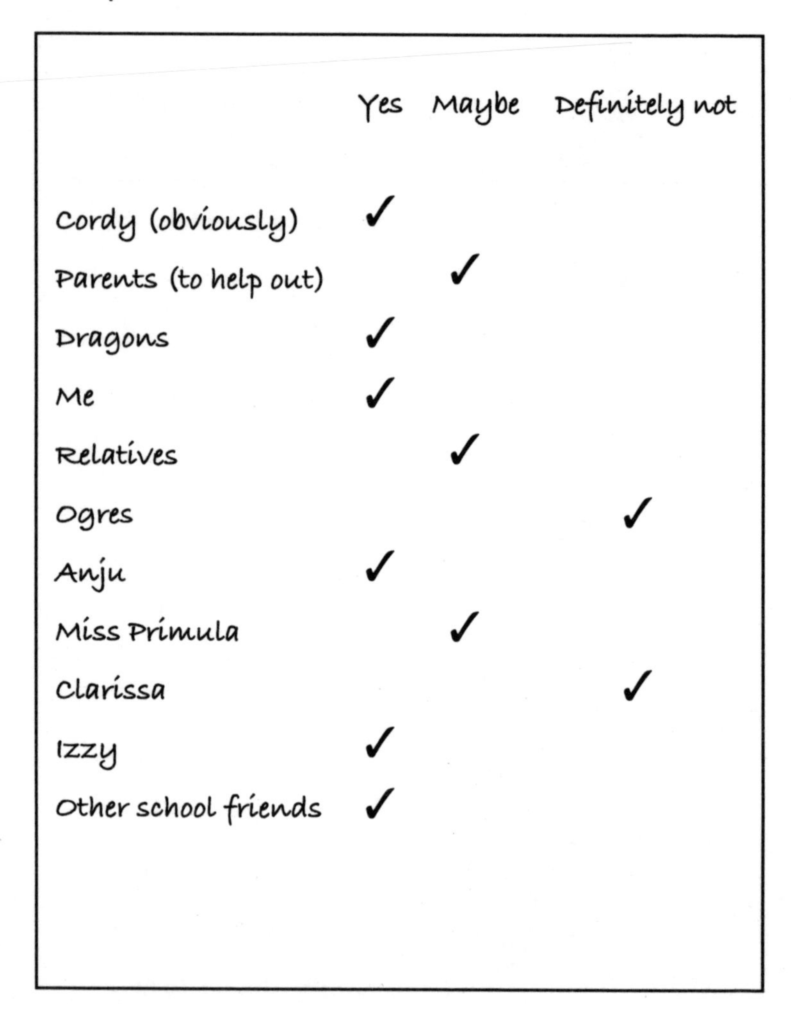

	Yes	Maybe	Definitely not
Cordy (obviously)	✓		
Parents (to help out)		✓	
Dragons	✓		
Me	✓		
Relatives		✓	
Ogres			✓
Anju	✓		
Miss Primula		✓	
Clarissa			✓
Izzy	✓		
Other school friends	✓		

We decide that maybe milkshakes and cookies in the park café might help the planning.

"I have designed an invitation," I say, showing Cordy a drawing.

"That's great!" she says.

"Maybe I should leave this with you to decide," I say, handing her the list.

Suddenly, my dad appears. And, as usual, he is taking pictures of himself.

"This is great!" he says as he takes a snap next to my chocolate muffin. "I'm now posting these online. Exhibitions are so old-fashioned. So I have created a blog: Cardigan Man about Town."

YES, IT'S
CARDIGAN MAN
ABOUT TOWN

PICTURES
OF ME IN
CARDIGANS!

CARDIGANS IN
FUNNY PLACES!

FUNNY
CARDIGANS IN
FUNNY PLACES!

"How many followers have you got?" asks Cordy.

"Eight!" says Dad proudly. "I'm getting chat, interaction ... people love it! I think I will need to get an agent. Someone to make this HUGE!"

"Well, eight of them love it," I whisper to Cordy. It turns out my dad knows all his followers by name (and six of them are in our family).

"News of this must never spread," I whisper to Cordy as I try to hide behind my milkshake. "Never."

The next day at school, everyone is crowded round a board in the playground.

"The school club lists are up!" shouts Izzy. "I'm in football, basketball and some other club I can't remember ..."

"I bet it involves a ball," says Cordy. We're playing it cool. There's only one club we're interested in, and it's not Mr Mavers's Plumbing Club.

We are being jostled all the way, but eventually we can read the sign. I carefully read the list for the

SCHOOL MAGAZINE CLUB.

"Cordy, you're in," I say. "So AM I! And Anju, and—*"

*I would rather not tell you one of the names who was also on the list, but I'm sure you can guess.

"I have BIG plans for the magazine." Clarissa says.

We all groan....

"Well, we've got BIGGER plans," I snap back (even though we don't actually have any plans yet).

But before we can start arguing about who has the plans for the magazine, the school bell rings and Ms Primula is ushering us into class.

Clubs start next week! I can hardly wait!

The next day, Miss Primula is talking to us about the childhood topic.

"Now, as you can see some people have done **really** well providing the classroom with material for the Memory Tree," she says, before saying a bit more sternly, "but some of you haven't brought anything in at all yet."

We are then led over to the tree to admire what is on there so far ...

Miss Hailey as a baby!

Anju eating her first cake (which she probably decorated herself)

Cordy's picture (The one with the scared looking fish)

TEN pictures of Clarissa (on expensive holidays, in expensive restaurants, and one with what looks like a golden dummy)

Izzy winning a football dribbling contest

AND OF COURSE: A **HUGE** GAP WHERE MY PICTURE SHOULD BE.

"In a couple of weeks we will be making the class trip to the Museum of Infancy," says Miss Primula. "And, as I said, I expect everyone to have brought in a picture of themselves by then!"

"Don't worry, no one will see them outside of this class," she adds.

I **HAVE** to get a picture of myself as a toddler. I will have to make another trip to Granny's, and soon!

I've managed to persuade my dad to drop me off at Granny's AGAIN and this time I have got to get a picture, no matter how embarrassing.

"I can't wait to see the cake!" says Cordy as she gives Granny a big bear hug. I have brought Cordy with me to help pick a picture.

"Not long now," says Granny as she recovers from Cordy's bear hug and gets her breath back.

"Now, what about those photos?" asks Cordy.

I know this is going to get embarrassing ...

"Oooh yes, follow me," chuckles Granny. "I've looked out a whole LOAD ..."

I now have to sit through a horrendous parade of pictures. Because, as well as being a champion cake baker, Granny is also the Orsen family's unofficial archivist.

"Let me see," says Granny as she takes an envelope out of an old shoe box. "I have hand-picked a selection of my favourites."

"Here is baby Beth being licked by a llama at a zoo ...

"Here she is falling into her birthday cake ...

"Oh, and this is my favourite, Beth riding a donkey at the beach ..."

For some reason Cordy and Granny find these photos hilarious. But there is no way I'm letting my class see these.

"Granny, I know you love these kind of pictures," I say, raising my eyebrows and widening my eyes in what I hope is a cute face. "I just wondered if you had any, you know, more straightforward ones. Just me, looking cute, maybe on a tricycle, that kind of thing ..."

"You mean BORING pictures," grumbles Granny as she looks at the very bottom of the box. "I suppose so – it's just everyone loves you in those other pictures."

Fortunately, Granny finds a few normal pictures – me in a high chair. Me with a kitten. She puts these in their own envelope.

"If you change your mind do come back and get the others," she chuckles. "Now, who would like a home-made MONSTER BROWNIE – it's the size of a small family car, and twice as tasty!"

We spend the rest of the afternoon discussing Cordy's party and I can't believe how quickly the time's passed when my dad arrives to take us home.

As we leave I realise I've forgotten the photos!

"I'll get them," says Dad, but as he goes into Granny's sitting room there is a horrendous commotion. He finally appears with the photos, but with his hair in a mess.

"Otto didn't seem too keen on letting these leave the house," gasps my dad as he brushes shredded paper from his shoulder. But with the photos in hand we are now on our way home.

It's after school and it's **CLUB NIGHT!**

In the past that would have meant doing something dreadful like trying to play basketball with a flat ball ...

Or guitar without music or strings ...

Or do art without paint ...

But not now – with Ms Hailey on the case, clubs are shaking and baking – **LITERALLY!**

There's Salsa Club and Home Cookery Club,

and, of course, **MAGAZINE CLUB**.

Cordy and I enter our classroom, which has been assigned to Magazine Club, to find a crowd already there – and **CLARISSA** sitting on the teacher's chair.

"Come in, come in," she says. "So nice of you to join me."

Once again it's Miss Primula to the rescue as she enters the room. "Thank you Clarissa, I think you'll find I'm in charge here," she says.

"But my dad …" protests Clarissa.

"We hugely value your father's kind offer to produce and print the magazine," says Miss Primula, "but I'm sure you'll agree we've got to be totally fair here."

"No, not really," says Clarissa, but Miss Primula isn't listening any more.

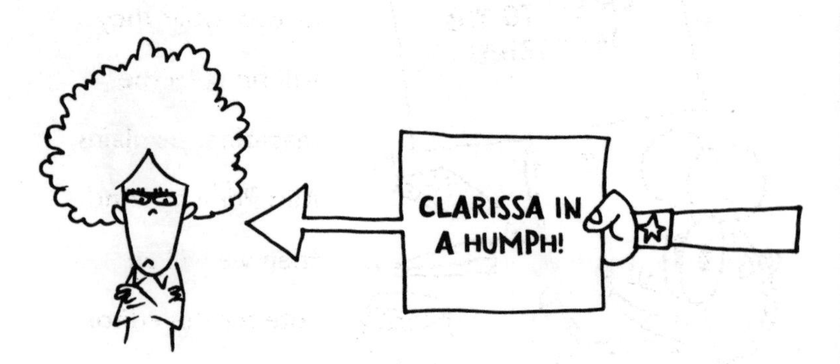

"So before we decide the stories we would like to cover, we need an editor and a deputy editor. It seems to me like the only fair way to do this is to have a vote ..."

A vote? We all wonder how this is going to work.

"Everyone has to say, in a sentence or two, what they will bring to the magazine," explains Miss Primula. "And then we will all vote for the editor and deputy editor."

One by one we each say what we'd put in the magazine:

"Lots of sport," says Izzy.

"Shopping and luxury holidays," says Clarissa.

"Cordy and I want to work together," I tell Miss Primula.

"OK," she says. "What would you two bring to the magazine?"

I know I have to say something utterly amazing. I need to capture the audience's imagination.

I need something they can believe in, something incredible but realistic. But, instead, I utter five words.

"An interview with Bobby Gothick."

It's a big promise, but I had to say something. When the hands are added up, my jaw hits the ground.

Because...

"Beth and Cordy! Congratulations, you're in charge!"

"I hope we can pull this off," whispers Cordy.

But I am too excited to think about how hard getting an interview with an A-list star might be. Right now this is the most exciting news EVER. I feel I should get up and make an emotional speech...

But fortunately I don't.

"I'll be supervising," says Miss Primula, "and to get the ball rolling I suggest we all think about story ideas over the weekend. We can then discuss them next week."

Never mind story ideas, Cordy and I will have to spend EVERY spare minute trying to get in touch with Bobby Gothick.

The next morning, Miss Primula has remembered the one remaining gap on the Memory Tree.

"Beth!" snaps Miss Primula in her 'listen up or I will unleash the dragon I keep in my bottom drawer'* kind of voice.

*I'm pretty sure there's a dragon in there – or at least a very hungry crocodile.

"There is STILL one spot left on our Memory Tree," she continues.

"Really?" I reply, trying to sound confused but not sounding confused at all. "A spot? What kind of a spot?"

"A Beth-sized spot," she half smiles. "Come on, you must have brought in something."

Luckily, I have the photos in my bag. As I hand them over I remind myself that they really aren't so bad (and they could have been so much worse!).

I give the envelope to Miss Primula ... but as she opens it my heart skips a beat, my ears wobble and I have a feeling of **HORROR** rush all over me (and it is not a nice feeling).

Because these aren't the right pictures! In fact, Miss Primula is now holding up **THAT PICTURE** ... the most **EMBARASSING** one of all – me on the donkey.

"What happened, Beth?" whispers Cordy. "I was there when your granny showed you the other pictures."

Then it comes back to me – my dad, Otto attacking him, the shredded paper ... he **MUST HAVE PICKED UP THE WRONG ENVELOPE!**

At first there is a chuckle, then a belly laugh then **THE WHOLE CLASS IS IN HYSTERICS** as Miss Primula attaches my picture to the tree.

I suppose you actually want to look at the picture ...

please notice the fact I have ICE CREAM smeared all over my face, I am CRYING, and finally that the donkey looks like it wants to cry, too.

"OK, calm down!" barks Miss Primula. "We should thank Beth for sharing her picture with us – you look like you were having lots of fun."

"I feel sorry for the donkey," pipes up Clarissa and once again the class falls about laughing.

"Enough! And of course the photo will only be seen by this class," Miss Primula adds as she looks at me.

My face is so **red** I don't think that it'll ever go back to its normal colour.

A few days later and I have **just** about recovered from the **terrible** photo mix-up. Cordy and I are working on the school magazine in our office. Well, I say 'office' but it's actually a corner of the school gym where Mr Musgrove has set up his high-tech printing machines.

We are drawing up plans – which is a fancy way of saying making a list. The school magazine needs to come out at the end of term and Cordy's birthday is also at the end of term. So we have lots to do!

"OK, so we need to make sure we get people writing about interesting things that are going on in school," I say as we start. "We also need some imaginative fun stuff."

"We must not allow Clarissa to take over," says Cordy.

But as we put our list together there is one REALLY big task that is looming over it. We need to find the front cover story.

"I think promising an interview with Bobby Gothick was a mistake," I sigh. "We have tried everything to get hold of him."

Having been through all the 'regular channels' – we have called the TV company, we have called the book publisher – we are now contemplating some 'irregular channels'.

So far I have suggested:

A poster being pulled behind a plane ...

Using a giant megaphone outside his house ...

And if that fails – Cordy and me dressing up as werewolves and hanging around on the film set ...

"Those ideas will never work," says Cordy, "even if dressing up as werewolves is fun ... we need something more sensible." But we can't think of anything.

At the moment it doesn't seem likely that we'll get the interview. What are we going to do?

Back home and I want to get to my room super quickly – with my head full of the school magazine, I have neglected Cordy's birthday planning and there's one particularly urgent task.

But getting to my room is proving to be impossible. No, there isn't a grumpy badger with bad breath sitting there. Even worse – it's my mum and she is armed to the back teeth

with ...

STAGE MAKE-UP!

"Just a quick dollop," she pleads, as she looms over me with a huge brush and a pot of red gloop.

My mum has done the first day of her course 'Stage and Screen Make-Up' at the School of Make-Up.

Yes apparently there really is a school of make-up.

I imagine everyone there is in full movie make-up ...

ALL THE TIME.

Using the magic of stage make-up ...

The head teacher looks like a **CAT!**

(So, not that different to Ms Hailey.)

The janitor is probably made up with a false beard and hairy eyebrows ...

And the school dinner ladies are probably all Egyptian mummies ...

It seems that the first day was all about warts, spots and unusual skin textures.

"Look at Bertie," says my mum, "he helped me out."

Bertie looks like he has a a slimy, MOULDY BLUEBERRY stuck to his face.

"That wart is pretty realistic, don't you think?" says Mum. "Now, if I could just put a TINY, WEENY, ULTRA SMALL SPOT OR WART ON YOU, BETH."

Luckily I slip around her and manage to get my bedroom door shut behind me.

I am finally in my room.

I have a theme for Cordy's party, I have a cake, I have sorted out most of the invitation list and I have even put Izzy in charge of party games (he will be so much better at that than me).

But there is one thing I'm missing. **A PRESENT FOR CORDY.**

Cordy is quite fussy and I know there have been some presents she **HATED**. She once got a set of pink pyjamas with pictures of ickle bicycles on from her grandma and her aunt Janine once bought her a cuddly toy rabbit.

I'm not going to get her something like that, but I don't know what to get her. The trouble is she has all the Dusk Light Saga stuff there is to buy, she has toy bats in every shape and size, and strawberry milkshakes don't last very long when they are wrapped up.

I need something UNIQUE and AMAZING – but what? Even Scribbles is out of ideas.

But before I can work out what, there is a shout from Dad ... it's dinner time.

"Hurry up, Beth, I need a quick dinner so I can get back to calling agents for Cardigan Man ..."

So, I **STILL** haven't got a present for Cordy. But I don't have time to shop because the next day it's school club night and it's now down to Cordy and me to outline our plans and get the first articles under way.

"We thought Anju could write a piece about the school art department," I say.

"And Izzy could be our sports reporter and write about how all the school teams have performed," says Cordy.

"That sounds great," says Miss Primula. "And what about you and your big suggestion?"

"Of course we will concentrate on the cover story – an interview with Bobby Gothick!" I say nervously. "Just as soon as we get in touch with him ..."

But Clarissa doesn't seem impressed.

"Guys, I think we can safely say the Bobby Gothick cover story is unlikely to happen," she starts. "I think we need a plan B."

"Plan B? No, never!"

I want to shout. But Miss Primula seems to want her to carry on.

"It's time to unveil MY big idea. Sooooo ... I thought, hey, why don't we make the first issue the *Clarissa* Issue?" she declares. Even Miss Primula looks slightly alarmed.

"I will write a feature about **MY** shopping trips ...

There will be a section on **ME** and **MY** holiday homes and on the cover ...

ME! ME! ME! ME! ME!

In **ALL** the latest fashions ..."

"Well, thank you for that, Clarissa, that sounds like a great back-up plan," says Miss Primula. "Of course we need to hear from our editor in terms of what works best for the magazine ..."

Fortunately, Cordy and I don't have to respond as we are interrupted by Clarissa's best friend, Desiree.

"Magazines are such hard work," she says in a happy voice. "So Clarissa's brought lemonade and cupcakes for everyone!"

I am about to say a warm, heartfelt thank you when I take a closer look at the icing on the top of the cake ...

"Is that ...?" I whisper to Cordy.

"Oh yes – only Clarissa would have pictures of herself on the icing of cupcakes," mutters Cordy. Like me, she seems to have lost her appetite.

"Thanks for the snacks, Clarissa," I start. "But we are still hopeful we'll get that interview, so we wondered if you'd be our columnist. You could write a, er, diary piece about a typical day in your life."

I can see Cordy giving me a 'seriously?' look, but it's better than Clarissa taking over the whole magazine.

"That's a great idea!" beams Miss Primula. "Now, I suggest we finish our cakes and start working on our articles!"

But Cordy and I can't just think about our articles. We have promised a major scoop! We need something and fast. It's then I remember that my dad mentioning getting an agent.

"We could try and talk to Bobby's agent," I say triumphantly. "We just need to find the address ..."

With a few clicks of the computer we have tracked down Bobby Gothick's agent.

"What is an Agent?" asks Cordy.

"My dad used to have an agent when he was a model. He now wants one for Cardigan Man. They look after contracts and money and other boring stuff," I say. "We get past the agent and we'll have our interview ..."

"I LOVE IT!" beams Cordy. "We just need the perfect time to pay her a visit."

"I know exactly when that will be." I smile as a plan starts to formulate in my mind.

For the first time since I mentioned it, I feel good about the Bobby Gothick interview. The school magazine is now full steam ahead!

We have sent reporters all over the school to come up with THRILLING, EXCITING stories and we know they are going to deliver.

Anju is ALL OVER the art room with Mrs Smudgely the art teacher.

She is getting up close with paintbrushes ...

Uncovering the secrets of the potter's wheel ...

And generally getting into the nitty-gritty of what makes the art department, well, so arty.

Meanwhile, sports reporter Izzy is getting all the exciting scoops from the school sports teams ...

He is checking out the school's top football striker (that happens to be him) ...

He is interviewing the school's leading basketball points scorer (also him) ...

And looking into the nooks and crannies of the school gym.

And Clarissa? Well, Clarissa seems to be **EVERYWHERE.** She has hired some fancy professional photographer – fortunately not my dad. And she seems to be getting enough material, **ABOUT HERSELF**, to fill not one but about 100 Clarissa Issues ...

"We need to remind her it's a two page 'Day in The Life' not an entire volume," I mutter to Cordy as Clarissa poses while the photographer snaps pictures of her in the school canteen.

With the school magazine taking great shape, finally the day arrives for the **school trip**

Everyone loves school trips, so when we gather at the school gates to visit the **Museum of Infancy** there is a general buzz in the air.

"This is going to be awesome," says Cordy, "especially with our little plan."

'Our little plan' is actually quite COMPLICATED.

It involves MY DAD, his SELFIE STICK and a SUB-TRIP to visit Philomena Flugg. Miss Primula has approved it all and Dad is meeting us after lunch.

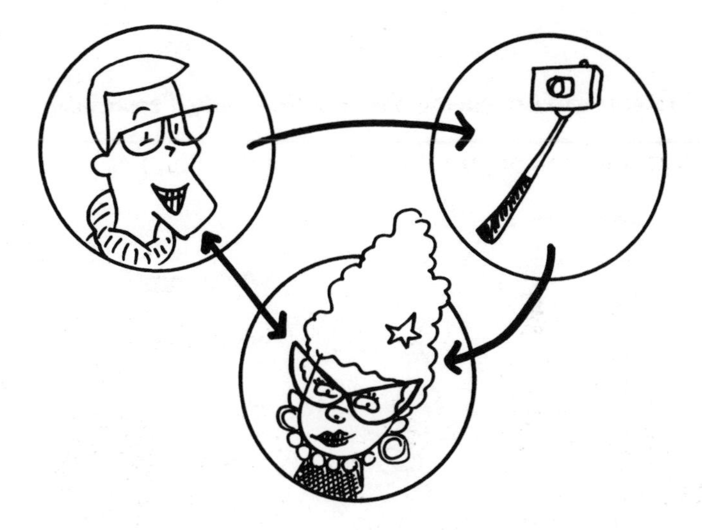

Are you following all this? I know, it's complicated.

But before any of that we have a school trip to go on, and the first stop is a walk to the train station as we are heading into town.

I love travelling by train – that is, until Clarissa sits right next to me. She has got wind of our plot (by listening in on our **PRIVATE** conversation) and has decided to stick her nose right in ...

"So you will be leaving the museum early, I hear," she says as she places her shiny pink handbag on her knees.

Whilst most of us have rucksacks, carrier bags and assorted sports bags Clarissa's bag is so frilly and fancy it looks like it might actually be a fairy house. Which gets my imagination going ...

In fact, what if we were on a fairy train driven by a leprechaun!

It's at times like this I wish I was a POWERFUL WIZARD. With a wave of my wand I would put Clarissa on a private train ...

A train with only one carriage ... and not heading to a normal destination. Because I would use my magic to create a track that would lead to a magical destination ...

And when the train got there, Clarissa would get off ... to discover the platform was made out of rotten eggs and they would RUIN her expensive shoes...

And a large smelly dog, with a slobbery tongue as long as a BUS, would appear and start to lick her LOVELY PINK BAG ...

Finally, giant red ants the size of CATS would crawl on her feet and she would get that horrible, annoying tickly feeling ...

I'm shaken out of my daydream as we finally arrive at our station. After a short walk we are at the museum.

Now, I am **NOT** like many people, who see a museum as...

And very much

3rd. The stuff in between.

I **like** the stuff in between – or the 'exhibits', to use the correct term – and the Museum of Infancy is full of great exhibits ...

Now, I would happily spend hours here, but school trips are always on a strict time limit. So we race all over the museum filling in answers on our questionnaires – it's a whir of pencils and clipboards.

Before we know it, it is LUNCH TIME.

"Are you ready to go?" I ask Cordy.

"Yes – we're going to make that front cover interview happen!" says Cordy.

For Cordy and me, it's time for our sub-trip to Philomena Flugg's office. We just need my dad to appear ...

Suddenly there is a loud commotion behind the **GIANT TEDDY** that sits in the middle of the museum café.

I should have guessed my dad wouldn't just slip in quietly.

"Hello, everybody!" roars Dad as he appears from behind the bear. "Who wants to be in a selfie with me?"

I wish the giant teddy would grab my dad and put him in a glass case full of creepy old dolls ... but no such luck.

"OK, Beth and Cordy," says Miss Primula. "I understand that your sub-trip is for the benefit of the school magazine. So good luck and make the school proud of you."

"This is **NOT** fair," wheedles Clarissa, her face going as pink as her pink bag. "I should be on this sub-trip trip. After all I ..."

But just then she spots the gift shop.

"OK, I've got shopping to do, I'll get back to you ..."

We are now in my dad's car heading to Philomena Flugg's office. I have given him STRICT orders not to sing while he's driving (which is one of Dad's most embarrassing habits), as Cordy and I need to be calm and relaxed when we meet her. I don't want my head full of my dad's jazzy version of 'The Wheels on the Bus'.

I have also told him to try to SECRETLY ask for a signed Bobby Gothick photo for Cordy's present.

"You know I might ask Ms Flugg if she needs any older actors," says my dad. "I could be in the movies ..."

I suddenly have a **horrible** picture in my mind:

CARDIGAN MAN – THE MOVIE

MIKE ORSEN STARS AS CARDIGAN MAN AS HE SOLVES CRIMES AND DEFEATS MONSTERS, ALL WEARING A CHUNKY-KNIT CARDIGAN!

Fortunately we arrive at the office and the image disappears. I make Dad promise NOT to mention Cardigan Man or acting.

Although Cordy and I are super-nervous, especially when we enter the office which is full of photos of the stars, Philomena is actually really nice.

"It's great to see two young people using their initiative," she says from behind her high desk. We feel quite small as we are sitting on low chairs.

"I wrote for my school magazine," she continues. "I wrote a piece about sausage rolls being introduced on the school menu, so I admire your ambition."

"Let me speak to Bobby," says Philomena Flugg. "He's very busy, but I think we can squeeze you in."

BOBBY GOTHICK IS ON THE PHONE!

Cordy and I are so excited that we lose track of the conversation.

"OK, he'll do it," says Philomena. "He'll call on the last Saturday of the month!"

Cordy and I look at each other in excitement. The magazine is meant to go to print the exact same day. It's going to be a rush, but we can do it!

"The cover story is in the bag!" I beam as we leave her office, but my smile soon turns upside down when I spot what my dad is doing.

"Hey guys, look – Cardigan Man is doing a selfie next to Philomena Flugg's water cooler!"

He was supposed to be asking for a signed photo for Cordy's birthday present! Now what am I going to get her?

So Cordy and I are back at school and in the gym. The magazine is nearly ready. The articles are all in, the pictures have arrived. The only thing missing is the **Bobby Gothick interview**. We know this will be last-minute so we'll put that in as soon as we've spoken to him on the phone.

Everyone else has gone home and we are now putting the final touches to the school magazine before it goes to print.

"I don't want to get too excited but I think it's going to be quite good," I say to Cordy in a quiet voice.

Miss Primula is also upbeat as she looks at our pages on the huge super-high-tech computer screens.

"I think there is something in this for everyone," she smiles. "Sport, art, teachers ..."

"And of course ME!"

booms a loud, gloating voice.

Clarissa still seems to thinks the magazine is all about

I FEEL QUEASY AGAIN!

"I'm sure our readers will be gripped by the **'DAY IN THE LIFE OF CLARISSA MUSGROVE'** section," says Miss Primula.

Here is a horrific sneak peak. Those with a sensitive disposition may want to skip this page ...

"I think I look **fabby-wabby**," gloats Clarissa. "But one there is one ickle thing missing, methinks ..."

Trust Clarissa to spot the tiny gap in the magazine. Well, I say tiny, but it's actually a gap so big you could drive a fork-lift truck through it. The front cover is completely empty! We are keeping it blank as we'll put a picture of Bobby Gothick there as soon as we have done the interview.

"Bobby Gothick will be giving us an interview on Saturday morning," I say, but I am quite nervous because:

The interview is scheduled for the day the magazine is being printed. Which is also Cordy's birthday!

PANIC – FEAR – MORE PANIC!

"And if he doesn't?" says Clarissa. "I think I know the perfect picture for the front cover ... me!"

"I'm sure Mr Gothick will help out if he promised to," interrupts Miss Primula. "Now, I think we all need to get home."

"We'd better hope Bobby Gothick gives us our interview," I complain to Cordy as we head home.

Cordy and I SHUDDER at the thought of Clarissa on the cover of our school magazine.

As the final few days pass, Cordy and I are also making the final plans for her birthday. In fact I'm so **frazzled** I don't notice that Scribbles has learned to play the bass and has formed a band with a couple of daddy-long-legs and a gnat.

Worryingly, there is no news about the Bobby Gothick interview, even though I have tried to call Philomena's office over **1,000 times**.

But when my dad stumbles into my room that finally gets my attention ...

He is battered and bruised and covered in blood!

"Dad! What happened?"

I exclaim.

"I was **mobbed** by screaming fans – my blog 'Cardigan Man About Town' has gone viral!" he moans.

For a second I think about calling an ambulance. But then I hear laughter as my mum, Bertie and even Mabel all come into my room.

"Got you!" says my mum. "I've completed my stage make-up course! Not bad, eh?"

"Not bad – it's amazing!" I say, seeing the funny side. I even stand next to my dad as he takes a selfie in his best crash-proof cardigan.

"Now I just need to keep practising," says Mum proudly. "Who's next?"

"Not now, but what are you doing Saturday afternoon, Mum?" I ask. I think I have just come up with a great idea for Cordy's birthday present.

"I'm around ..." says my mum, wondering what I'm getting at.

"You're going to need your make-up skills," I say, with a grin. "I've got a stage make-up job for you!"

It's finally arrived; Saturday, the day of Cordy's zombie birthday party – **yippee!**

Everything is ready to go … Cordy's mum is decorating the park, my dad is setting up the barbecue, Granny will be delivering the cake, the guests have all said they are coming.*

It's going to be

AWESOME!

*Whoops! I seem to have broken the first rule from my birthday guide – the one about no parents!

But before the party, Cordy and I ... are in **SCHOOL**. (Yes, it's one of my **STUPIDLY BUSY DAYS!**)

"I always assumed that on Saturdays the school was overrun with the ghosts of children from hundreds of years ago," Cordy says in a creepy voice. "Playing old-fashioned games and running up and down the corridors."

"You could write a piece about it for the next school magazine," I reply. "It would have been good if we'd had some more creative writing stories ..."

"I think you'll find we still have some work to do on *this* edition," says Miss Primula, who is helping out.

Yes, I know it's the weekend, and **yes** I know it's Cordy's birthday but right now we have important work to do,

SPECIFICALLY

interviewing Bobby Gothick. It's super last-minute but Philomena did say he would call. If not, the front page will be Clarissa, the centre spread pages all Clarissary! **THIS IS THE SITUATION WE HAVE BEEN DREADING!**

But right now
we are staring,
and waiting,
and waiting,
and staring
at a phone
that refuses
to ring ...

"Nothing, nada, not a peep," I sigh as the phone continues **NOT** to ring.

"Philomena said Bobby would call today ..." groans Cordy, glancing at the gym clock.

The phone just refuses to ring.

"I'm sorry, guys, but I think we're just about out of time," says Miss Primula. "We'll just have to go with the alternative cover and story."

This is 

.

"That means we're really going to be stuck with the Clarissa Issue!" I wail in a panicked voice.

"Isn't there something else we can do?" implores Cordy.

"We've run out of time," says Miss Primula. "Mr Musgrove will be here any minute to print the magazine and he needs his machines back. And we have to go to the park for Cordy's party."

"You did your best," Miss Primula adds.

"We'll get Bobby Gothick on the cover of the next magazine," says Cordy gloomily.

"Along with your story about how school is haunted at the weekend." says Miss Primula, as she starts to tap away at the main computer.

In the blink of an eye every screen has Clarissa's face beaming down from it. I try to lift the mood.

"Well, I've got a big surprise present for you when we get to the park!" I say. I am now seriously determined to make this day **EXTRA BRILLIANT** from now on.

Miss Primula walks us to the park.

Cordy is **DESPERATE** to find out what my surprise is, but her guesses are ludicrous.

"I know – you've hired a stage set from Dusk Light and transformed the whole park into a Transylvanian castle?"

"Er, no ..." I reply.

"No, wait," says Cordy. "You've built a giant animatronic troll that will lift us up to the clouds?"

"Definitely not," I chuckle as we arrive at the park.

But when we arrive we are blown away. **THE PARK LOOKS AMAZING!**

The table is a giant COFFIN.

The chairs have all been decorated to look like tombstones.

There are spray cobwebs over the presents.

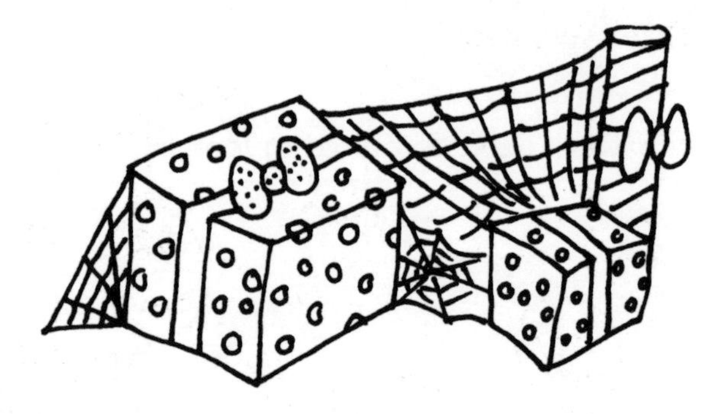

And there are sweets and chocolates shaped like eyeballs and fingers.

Even the barbecue has a zombie twist ...

Some of the guests are already there and Cordy's family and the team have done a great job of giving everything a zombie theme.

"It's so much better than I imagined it would be!" says Cordy. "Thank you, Beth."

"I got a lot of help," I say, but as I look around I feel quite pleased with myself.

"Wow, this place is amazing!" beams Cordy.

"But that's not the surprise!" I say. "Mum!"

My mum now appears from behind a coffin – looking like a **ZOMBIE!**

From all over the park, zombies appear, more and more of them shuffling towards us.

Even though I recognize Izzy in a ripped-up zombie football kit, Anju with a bloodstained false arm and Zach, who looks like his leg has dropped off, it's actually a bit scary. But when I glance at Cordy, she's grinning in delight.

"This is **AWESOME!**" she squeals.

Mum reaches us.

"I've been expecting you," she croaks in her scary voice. "Are you ready?"

"Surprise! Mum is going to make us both up to look like **PROPER** zombies!"

This is **GREAT** and my mum is soon getting to work on the two of us.

"You're really good, Mrs Orsen," says Cordy as she occasionally glances into a mirror.

"A bit too good," says Anju, who is cowering behind a shrub.

Soon we both look like zombies and can join in the party. The gathering clouds only add to the atmosphere.

Izzy, who organised the zombie games, has done a brilliant job.

We're soon playing a game of zombie football (with a papier mâché head for a ball). And birthday girl Cordy scores the winning goal.

I'm having so much fun I have almost forgotten about the school magazine and the **'Clarissa Issue'**.

After a break for BLOOD (blackcurrant squash), BRAIN JUICE SANDWICHES (actually chocolate spread), and FRESH ROADKILL (pepperoni pizzas) we're ready to play some more.

"Time for a new game," suggests Izzy. "Let's play Zombie Tag!"

"That sounds good," says Cordy. "So, what are the rules?"

"I've got this skull and crossbones flag," says Izzy. "We chase whoever has the flag ..."

But I have stopped listening because I have spotted someone entering the park.

It's pink. It's creepy.

"I'm a Zombie Fairy! Check out the outfit!" grins Clarissa. "I invented the character myself! Not only that but I had the costume made by my mummy's favourite designer."

"Sorry, Beth," whispers Cordy, "I should have warned you, my mum insisted on inviting her. Let's not let her spoil the fun. Now you enjoy yourself while I fetch everyone an EYEBALL LOLLY."

I try to grin. I try to avoid her. But it doesn't work, and

with Cordy off the scene I am soon cornered. Clarissa seems determined to spoil my fun.

But nothing prepares me for what she's about to say:

"Oh, Beth, there was a last-minute change to the magazine cover," she drops in casually. My blood turns colder than a ZOMBIE BLOOD MILKSHAKE IN A FREEZER.

"Yes I'm FAR too modest to be on the cover," she continues.

"I thought **YOU** should be on it instead ..."

My head goes a bit woozy – this is not going to be good ...

"I thought your baby picture would be perfect for the cover," she finishes. "And some of your other pictures are inside. It's going to print, right about ... NOW! Enjoy!"

"But it's now the Clarissa Issue," I babble. "How does my picture even fit in?"

"Oh yes, it's 100% still the Clarissa Issue," she smiles. "The headline reads: Meet Baby Beth Orsen – someone who Clarissa knows."

I am frozen to the spot when I hear another familiar voice. But this time it's a voice I do like.

"Beth!" says the voice. "Look at my masterpiece ...

But as I spin round I bump into the person speaking. Everything seems to go a bit slow motion. My arms flail madly. There is a blur of green. And then ...

SPLAT!

My head goes all squelchy as a large, soft blob lands on me. All I can see is something green and spongy.

I squint through the mush on my head.

"Granny?" I exclaim.

"My Zombie Cake!" shrieks Granny.

I CANNOT BELIEVE WHAT I'VE DONE!

All of that work.

All of those scrummy ingredients.

All over **ME!!!**

It's a

CAKE-TASTROPHE!

I've knocked Granny's cake in the air and most of it seems to have landed on my face. The huge cake is wrecked, and I am covered in sugary green slime.

"Are you OK, Beth?" asks Granny.

"Yes," I reply, "I'm SO sorry," I apologise.

"Granny, I can't talk ..." I babble through a face full of cake. "Got to get to school ..."

I would **love** to help Granny pick up the cake, I would **love** to apologise to her and Cordy but I **need** to stop the school magazine from printing.

As I rush off, I feel something on my back, but I ignore it as I run past Cordy.

"Cordy, I've got to go!" I shout. "Magazine emergency."

But Cordy is having too much fun with all the others to listen.

"Get her!" she yells.
"I'll be back,"
I call over my shoulder.
But as I glance around, I see all the others – and they're chasing me!

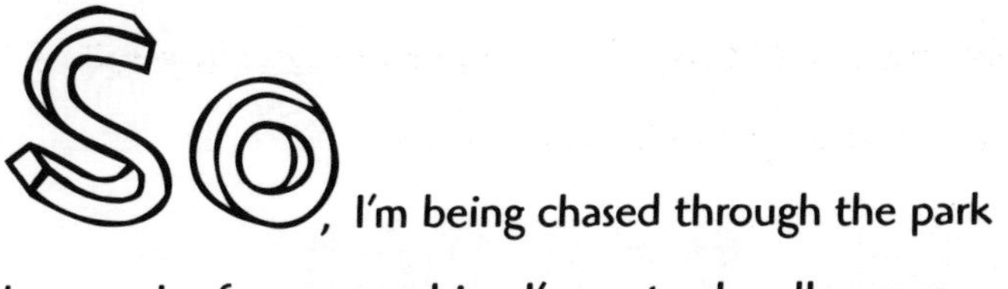

So, I'm being chased through the park by a pack of angry zombies, I've got cake all over my face

AND MY MOST **EMBARRASSING** PHOTO EVER IS ABOUT TO APPEAR IN THE SCHOOL MAGAZINE!!!

But I have no time to clean up or get changed because I am now on ...

OPERATION STOP THE SCHOOL MAGAZINE FROM BEING PRINTED!!!

I need to get to the school. But the pack of zombies, led by Cordy, will not leave me alone. In fact, the faster I go the faster they go ...

"Guys, back off!" I screech – but they just find this hilarious.

"This zombie has attitude!" chuckles Anju.

There is now a flash of lightning and a crack of thunder. There are excited shrieks from behind me. The zombies, especially Cordy, are loving it!

I run around in a circle and they STILL won't leave me alone. I FINALLY work out what's going on – I have Izzy's flag pinned to my back – everyone thinks I'm playing Zombie Tag.

I try and pull the flag off my back but I can't reach it. Looks like I will be taking the whole zombie party with me to the school.

I finally arrive at the school and manage to get inside. As I shut the doors, Anju trips and Cordy drops her eyeball ice lolly. Finally, all the zombies stop.

Alone, I burst through the doors of the school gym. There are whirring noises coming from the machines in the corner. The printing is about to start. I need to find Mr Musgrove, and fast ...

"Mr Musgrove! Mr Musgrove!

YOO-HOO!" I yell.

"What's happened to you?" cackles Mr Musgrove as he observes the sponge that is stuck to my face. "Beth, I do believe I really have now seen it all!"

"Oh yes, it's a long story," I say, looking down at my cake-splattered outfit.

"You are **hilar-i-ous**," says Mr Musgrove. "And just you wait until you see your picture on the front of the magazine. Fabulous! You know, Beth, I laughed so much I almost fell off my executive swivel chair ..."

"That's great ... It's just I need you to stop printing the school magazine, at once!" I gasp as I see my picture on the screen.

MAGAZINE
Meet baby
Beth Orsen -
someone who
CLARISSA
knows!

"No can do," says Mr Musgrove. "The machines are set. It's an expensive business, printing magazines, and as far as I'm concerned this is the finished product. And besides, I need to pick up Clarissa and then go to the golf club ..."

"But you don't understand ..." I beg.

"No time," says Mr Musgrove as he puts his jacket on. "If you stand here the magazines will start running off in a minute or two. You will be the first person to see one 'in the flesh'. Or should that be 'in the paper'?"

He then laughs a horse-like laugh which reminds me of someone – oh, yes, his daughter Clarissa.

As Mr Musgrove starts to head for the exit, my mind is whirring. Half of my brain is thinking about what I will do when the magazine is printed. So far the options are:

1. Move to a desert island, live on coconuts and hopefully befriend a local crab ...

or

2. Live in an enchanted tower in the middle of an enchanted forest where absolutely no one I know can reach me ...
or, better still
3. Live in an enchanted tower on a desert island ...

The other half of my brain is trying to work out any last-minute solutions to stop the magazine from printing.
So far my options are …

1. Call up the jam monster to smear super-juicy jam on the machines

Or

2. Cover Mr Musgrove in cake

Or

3. I'm so confused I don't even have an option 3!

But as my brain whirs, so do the machines and Mr Musgrove is rapidly approaching the exit door of the gym …

Which suddenly swings open!

"Mr Musgrove, look! It's zombies! Get a picture! *That* can go on the cover of the magazine!" I shout in despair.

"YIKES!" screeches Mr Musgrove as he is startled by the arrival. "Those zombies are far too realistic!"

"It's only me, Cordy," says the lead zombie.

"And I'm Izzy," says another zombie.

But Mr Musgrove has seen enough and runs out of the gym in a hurry.

Miss Primula now arrives – she had followed the crowd of zombies out of the park. As soon as I explain how Clarissa switched the pictures she stops the printing at once.

"This is **GREAT** news," I sigh. I take the old photo of me and put it in an inner, inner, inner secret pocket. "When Granny gets this back she'll have to promise never to show it to anyone ever again."

"We have a front cover and story to do," I say. "I don't think Bobby Gothick is going to save the day."

"Well, we need something – and fast," adds Miss Primula. "And the Clarissa Issue is cancelled!"

Suddenly I have ANOTHER brainwave. (I'm having A LOT of brainwaves lately, it must be something in Granny's cakes.)

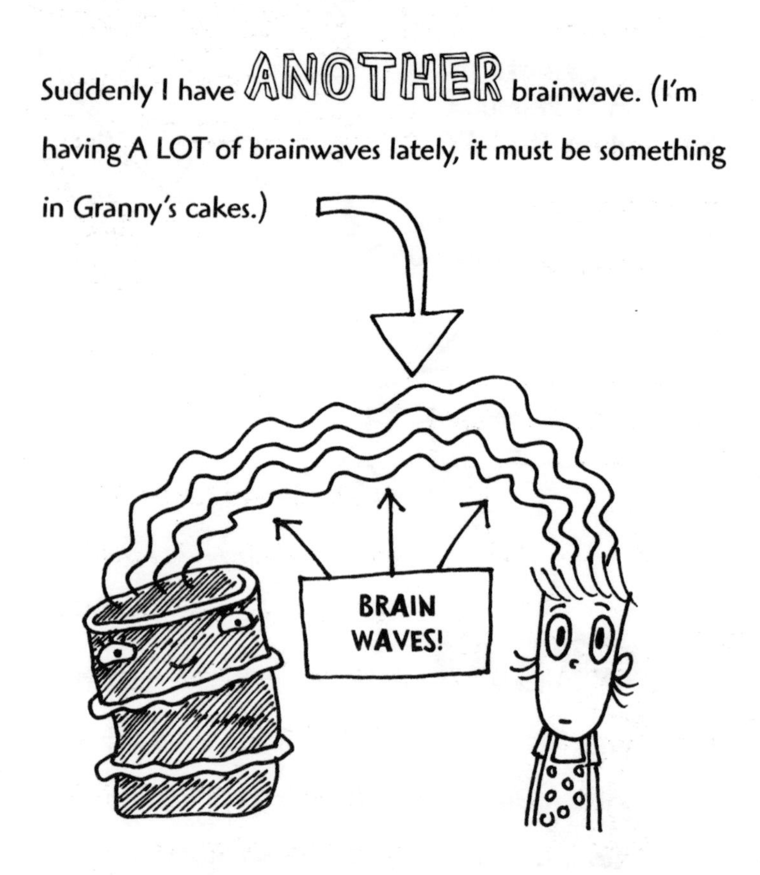

"Look outside, it's starting to rain ..." says Miss Primula.

"Do you think we could relocate Cordy's party indoors, here in the school gym?" I ask in my most sensible voice.

"Well, I'd have to check with Ms Hailey – it would be highly unusual," says Miss Primula, "but given that we were here for the school magazine anyway, I think it would be OK to ask."

In no time Miss Primula has got the
all-clear for the school gym to be used and the school is now overrun by zombies.

"This is perfect," Cordy whispers to me. "It's the best birthday ever ..."

"Well, there's more," I say. "I'm going to get my dad to take some pictures ..."

"Pictures?" says Cordy.

"For the school magazine, of course," I reply. "I've had the PERFECT idea for a fun new cover story...

You need to get writing. I need that story about the school being used at the weekends – by zombies!

"Dad, please start snapping," I say to my dad. "And please, no cardigan selfies – they just won't work for the headline."

My dad is now all over the party, taking pictures of zombies in the gym, zombies in the classroom – even a zombie head teacher in her office (Ms Hailey has arrived and she NEVER turns down the chance to dress up.) And best of all, no Clarissa!

When my dad has finally taken the last picture we all sing HAPPY BIRTHDAY to Cordy and eat some of the zombie cake that Granny has managed to salvage.

"Don't worry, Cordy," says Granny. "I'll bake you another one next year. I actually think I can make that green icing even scrummier!"

Cordy and I – along with Miss Primula – take a quick break from the party to put the finishing touches to the school magazine.

A few days later and I am at home hanging out with Cordy. We are admiring our amazing handiwork.

ZOMBIE SCHOOL INVASION!!!
A brand-new original story about how terrifying zombies roam YOUR school at the weekends!

"And look – we even mention the Clarissa pages," I say.

"In such ickle teeny letters you would need a microscope to see them," laughs Cordy.

"I admit, they're tiny," I agree, "but then we know what our readers really want – **ZOMBIES!**"

Just then there is a knock at the door – it's Mabel, so this can only mean BAD NEWS. But strangely (and worryingly) she is smiling ...

"You'll never believe who has come to visit you," she says. "Only Bobby Gothick!"

Cordy and I stare at each other, our eyes popping like real zombies!

And there, in front of us, is the gorgeous hero of the Dusk Light movies.

"Hey guys," says the Hollywood megastar, "I'm so sorry I didn't call you. I heard all about you from Philomena and just **HAD** to meet you both ..."

We don't know what to say. I gasp. Cordy really **GASPS**. I stutter. Cordy really **STUTTERS**.

Then I notice it.

"So Bobby, do you dress yourself or do you have a stylist?" I quiz the grinning heartthrob.

"Beth," hisses Cordy. "What are you talking about?"

"It's just that I don't think A-list stars wear CARDIGANS!" I proclaim.

Suddenly Cordy sees what I see – the wig, the make-up – the cardigan. It's Dad!

"You can come in, Mum," I continue as my mother enters the room, her make-up bag in hand.

"You've got a bit too good, Mrs Orsen," says Cordy, looking slightly disappointed.

"Yes, and can you now please leave us alone to WALLOW in our school magazine triumph," I say as I usher my family towards the door.

But just then my dad's phone rings.

"Yes, they are here and they would love to speak to you ..." says my dad. "Girls, say hello to Bobby Gothick ..."

"Whatever, Mr Orsen, we're not falling for that again," Cordy scoffs.

But behind all the make-up, I can see my dad's serious face. Which can only mean one thing ...

BOBBY GOTHICK IS ACTUALLY ON THE PHONE!

Swoon, swoon, super-swoon!

"Sure, I'd love to be on the cover of your next magazine!" drawls the movie star. "And Cordy, I believe I owe you a signed photo!"

"Now, that has got to be worth a selfie!" says my dad.

My latest adventure is finally over and with a happy ending. But my blood freezes when Cordy makes a suggestion.

"Hey, why don't we start planning *your* BETHDAY?"

I think I've had enough birthday adventures for a while!

FIND OUT MORE ABOUT ME AT
www.knifeandpacker.com